SAILING

BASICS TO CRUISING

ALSO

HOW TO MAKE MONEY
WITH YOUR BOAT

BY

KERR ROBINSON

WINDRIFT PUBLISHING
PETALUMA, CA

Printed in the United States of America

Edited and formatted by Linda Scantlebury, www.we-edit.com
Cover design by Linda Scantlebury, www.we-edit.com
Photos by Kerr Robinson
Cartoons by Andrew Fox

ISBN 0-9759207-0-7

Published by Windrift Publishing
2501 Stony Point Road
Petaluma, CA 94952
(707) 792-9974

This book is dedicated to my wife, Mary. Without her encouragement it would not have been written.

To my son Steven, who made much of my cruising more interesting. Who else in the world ever had a wild frigate bird swoop down and land on his upturned palm, stay for some minutes, then fly away again to soar the heavens.

To my sister Doris, who has been helping me since birth.

And to my best friend, Jozo, who assisted so ably on my first ocean crossing.

CONTENTS

PART THREE: HOW TO MAKE MONEY WITH YOUR BOAT

With sincere thanks to Andrew Fox for all the cartoon drawings. Though Andrew was in the midst of his Master's finals, he found time to cram in a lot of fine sketches.

Part One

The Basics

THE CALL OF THE SEA

I must go down to the seas again, to the lonely sea and the sky,
And all I ask is a tall ship and a star to steer her by,
And the wheel's kick and the wind's song and the white sail's shaking,
And a gray mist on the sea's face and a gray dawn breaking.

I must go down to the seas again, for the call of the running tide
Is a wild call and a clear call that may not be denied,
And all I ask is a windy day with the white clouds flying,
And the flung spray and the blown spume, and the seagulls crying.

I must go down to the seas again, to the vagrant gypsy life,
To the gull's way and the whale's way, where the wind's like a
whetted knife,
And all I ask is a merry yarn from a laughing fellow rover,
And quiet sleep and a sweet dream when the long trick's over.

"Sea Fever," by John Masefield

This poem by John Masefield was a required memorization study in public elementary school, and henceforth created many hours of daydreaming for me. The call of the sea is heard by many people and responded to in various ways. Since the first sailor, a prehistoric man or woman, straddled a log and paddled around, mankind has spent countless hours, even lifetimes, developing watercraft: from dug-out logs, later with outriggers added for stability; skin–covered frames of the American Indian's canoe and the Eskimo's kayak; the Irish coracle, which resembled a great round basket; to the modern

3

hi-tech ultra-light racing sailboats and power boats which attain unbelievable speeds.

A person who enjoys being on the water doesn't need a large, expensive yacht, but can enjoy puttering around in even the smallest rowing boat, sailboat, or inflatable dinghy. In fact, one of the most enjoyable occupations is "gunkholing," which is simply exploring a harbor, river, yacht basin, or any place you can reach in a small watercraft.

Sailing has been described as resembling standing in a cold shower tearing up dollar bills. However, something magical happens when the sails are hauled up, the motor is shut down, the sails take over, and you glide along silently, faster, and with more power than you had with the noisy engine running. Now you can go anywhere you wish in the whole wide world, sailing the seven seas, providing you have enough food and water on board.

Whether your taste is sailing or power boating, either is a wonderful way to escape from the rat race. Your watercraft may be a small boat with an outboard motor, a small sailing dinghy with a simple, one-sail rig, or a large mega-yacht with every conceivable convenience, such as water makers, generator sets, bow thrusters, stern thrusters, automatic stabilizers, air conditioners, hot tubs, worldwide telecommunications, helicopter pads, and so on. Boating in any form is still one of the last frontiers, and a wonderful escape from the everyday world. Actually, it appears that the smaller the boat, the more it leaves its berth. Many large yachts seldom leave their berths, since they are used more for entertaining than sailing.

Learning Boat Handling 1

When one buys the first boat it is important to learn as much as possible about that boat and how to handle her. The Power Squadrons, a branch of the United States Coast Guard, offer free classes; even people who have been boating for years can learn a lot from these courses, which cover everything you need to know to get started. You will learn the rules of the road (of the utmost importance); anchoring; and how much scope, line or chain, to let out. You can learn course plotting, how to read a chart, and how to allow for current and tidal drift, and so forth.

Often the reason a person loses interest in his boat is that he or she has never learned how to control it and consequently is uncomfortable, if not afraid, to take it out of the berth or bring it back in. The whole process of using the boat then becomes a real chore instead of a great pleasure.

The first thing you need to practice when learning proper boat handling is turning around and accomplishing a 180-degree course change without having to move much either forward or backward. Single-engine inboard boats tend to back up, pulling the stern to one side or the other, which makes handling them difficult. Most engines are installed at a slant, with the front of the engine higher than the rear, making the propeller shaft also slant down toward the rear. This slanted propeller shaft moving through the water horizontally gives the propeller more pitch on one side than the other; consequently, a right hand prop will pull the stern to the left or port side, and a left-hand prop will pull the stern to the right or starboard side. In a deep-draft vessel where the propeller shaft is installed horizontal or parallel to the water line there will not be any adverse pulling to one side or the other.

So the first thing to learn is what tendency your boat has; often you can use this to your advantage and it will assist you in turning your boat around in its own length. If your boat, when backing, pulls to the left or port side, you will learn that it is easier to make a turn to the right, swinging the bow to starboard.

To practice, have the boat stationary in the water and turn the steering wheel to the right or the tiller of a sailboat to the left, which will put the rudder over to the right to make the bow swing to the right. Put the gear shift into forward gear and give it a little throttle, but just as the boat starts to move forward, shift into reverse and gun it a little to stop the forward movement. Then just as you start moving backward, go back into forward gear and gun it to check the rearward movement. All this time you still have the wheel hard over to starboard. There is no need to move the wheel as you continue the back and forward gearing. You will continue your swing around to starboard until you are facing the desired course. Straighten the wheel to amidships and you are on your way.

This sounds a complicated thing to do at first, but once you have mastered this fairly simple technique, you will be more confident. You will be able to enjoy taking your boat into any little harbor. As long as the area is wider than the length of your boat, you will be able to turn around and get back out again.

There is always, however, the possibility that the wind will be blowing, and if you have to maneuver in close quarters, you have to take this into consideration. If the wind is blowing from the left, you have to stay well to the left side of your turning area and not let yourself be blown down into a downwind corner, from which it may be more difficult to escape.

When first learning boat handling, you don't need to practice in the harbor with lots of eyes watching your every move. Instead, you can move away to open water with lots of space around you, and there you can make a simulated berth by throwing out four plastic gallon bottles almost filled with water. These will float deep in the water and not blow away. You will need to weight them with a lead sinker if the wind is strong, to hold them firmly in the water but still floating. Place these bottles one in each corner of a large square or rectangle the shape of your berth; then you can drive your boat into this area from different angles, stopping in the marked area. Do this over and over again, sometimes backing in, also watching the wind direction and how it affects you, and pretty soon you will be able to put your boat exactly where you want to.

After a few days of this practice, you will know exactly how your boat reacts to all the variables, and you will not be at all hesitant about taking your boat out; in fact, you may be the envy of many of those who watch you bring her back into your berth like a real professional skipper.

Many people buy their boat and feel that, well, it has a steering wheel, a gearshift, and a throttle, somewhat resembling an automobile. However, boats do not handle like cars—they drift sideways and every which way, moved by the current or tide and the wind. This really complicates things. It takes practice to get used to these variables, so take the time to practice and you will really enjoy boating and getting away from it all.

They say that the two happiest days in a person's life are the day you buy your first boat and the day you sell it. I think this saying refers to those who never take the trouble to get comfortable with their boat. So take the time to really learn boat handling; then you will be a happy, competent skipper and be sad when it comes time to sell her.

SAILING 2

Mankind has been building sailing craft for thousands of years. And the wonderful thing about a sailing yacht is that there is no limit to where you can go. However, there is a problem if you want to go directly from A to B and the wind is blowing directly from B to A. With an inefficient sailing craft like a raft, with no keel, it will not be possible to get there. But Thor Hyardahl proved with Kon-Tiki, and later with the reed boat Raa, that primitive people, even in very inefficient sailing craft, could and did travel thousands of miles across the oceans of the world.

Before I went sailing for the first time, I just couldn't figure how sailboats could make way against the wind. Actually they cannot make headway directly against the wind; there is an area of approximately forty-five degrees on each side of the wind into which they cannot sail. Modern racing sailboats can sail closer than forty-five degrees, but heavy cruising boats are lucky if they can make or beat the forty-five-degree angle.

By hauling the sails in as flat as possible and sailing "close hauled" with a keel to keep you from going sideways, you can tack back and forward in a zigzag course up into the wind until you finally arrive at your destination, even if the destination is upwind. In the remaining three-quarters of the compass, you can set your sails to go in any direction you wish.

The first time a person goes sailing, it is a shock to feel the boat lean over, its sails pressed by the wind, until you are convinced that it is going to turn turtle and dump you in the water. A small sailboat, with or without a heavy keel, can be pressed over so far that the skipper must ease out the mainsail and round up into the wind. This will immediately bring the boat upright. For this reason, a small sailboat should never have the sheets (the ropes that control the set of the sail) tied or cleated firmly. This will make it difficult to release or ease out the sails in a hurry when the boat is being hard pressed by the wind.

A sailboat is, however, a very safe craft, and if she has a deep keel and the right sails set, the wind will drive her along with no problems. Relatively small sailboats have survived hurricanes and typhoons at sea that have sunk large ships in the same area. As the wind leans the boat over, the wind starts to spill out of the sails, and it takes more wind to make it lean over more, which in turn spills more wind out of the sails; consequently, it takes much more wind to push the mast over. If he is going out on a very windy day, a concerned skipper will shorten sail by reefing the regular sails or putting up smaller or storm sails, or by using fewer sails than the normally designed sail plan calls for.

ACQUIRING YOUR BOAT 3

Once you decide to buy a boat, the fun of looking at boats begins. It's even fun just walking around yacht harbors and studying every boat, whether she's for sale or not. Going to boat shows is also lots of fun, with boats of every shape and size on display: sailboats, houseboats, drifters, dinghies and inflatable. You can see all types of marine gear, engines, outboards, and electronic equipment. In fact, the larger boat shows have almost every conceivable watercraft made. There are even beautiful, gleaming ski-boats, jet-skis, or wave riders, which resemble a water-type motorcycle.

Usually manufacturers extend discounts on purchases made during the show, and give all kinds of incentives to get you to buy. Even though they have a listed price, you can always write up an offer, and this is a starting place. I was, at one time, a yacht salesman, and at a boat show where our company had seven different sailboats on display, I was pleased when an interested gentleman asked me to write up an offer on a 30-foot boat. The offer was almost 30 percent less than our special boat show price, but I wrote it up anyway. After much haggling, with no movement on the part of the buyer at all, I was amazed to see my boss accept the deal; the new buyer had made a real bargain buy.

You may be lucky to be looking to purchase in a buyer's market. Whether you are buying a new or used boat from a dealer or yacht salesman, or dealing directly with a private owner, you can always make an offer based on what you think the boat is worth or what your maximum investment has to be, even if the yacht is priced much higher. The owner may say absolutely not, but give him your name and phone number, and you never know—you may just hear from him in a few days.

I once saw a 37-foot sailboat that a young couple had fallen in love with but couldn't afford, since they were limited to a maximum investment of $37,500.00. They wanted to quit their jobs and sail off to the South Seas, so they couldn't pay more than the amount they had set aside for the boat. Getting a loan was out of the question, as they would be cruising, with no money coming in to make payments. They were negotiating with a private party who was asking $70,000.00 for the boat.

When the couple made the offer, they apologized that they could not offer more, and when the seller flatly refused to sell, they left him with their phone number, in case he changed his mind. A few days later the owner called them and told them to bring a cashier's check. He had not been using the boat; it was dirty and neglected and didn't show well, and he was tired of paying the berth rental every month.

So, you never know. Make an offer. You can always come up in price, but it is difficult to lower your offer.

Unless you are extremely knowledgeable about boats and how they are constructed, it is necessary to make the offer subject to your obtaining an up-to-date survey by a professional marine surveyor. For a relatively small fee, he will examine almost every detail regarding condition, construction, etc., also repairs that are needed or recommended. He will also tell you his opinion of the value of the boat, and what it would cost to duplicate the building of it today. It may be an older wooden boat no longer manufactured and very expensive to repair or duplicate.

You will receive a very detailed written report. If the report is good, you can feel optimistic about going ahead with the deal. If the survey uncovers faults and give recommendations and the approximate costs of these necessary repairs or changes, and if you still want to buy the boat, then you have the knowledge on which to base a new offer or make the seller correct the problems, if that is possible.

Of course, marine surveyors are human and not infallible. They cannot see through materials that may hide faults; they may miss something in their survey. Nevertheless, the fee charged for their services is well worth the expense, for the knowledge you gain from their experience. It is important to enlist every aid to help you buy at the right price, so have the boat surveyed.

Consider that it is possible to buy an older fixer-upper cheap, or even get her for nothing, and yet have made a bad deal. The costs of restoring iher may far exceed the figure for which you could have purchased a same-sized yacht in good, turnkey condition.

Good boats can be very expensive, so it is well worth taking the time to find just the right one for your purposes. Remember the old saying that the two happiest days in a man's life are the day he buys his first boat and the day he sells it? This means that there are always lots of boats for sale.

CAN'T FIND THE RIGHT BOAT? BUILD IT!

Building boats for sale is possible, though it requires an investment in quite a lot of tools and equipment, also a yard, preferably near the water or within launching distance of water. This can also be a long time commitment, which may not be what you are interested in, especially if you have broken away from the humdrum of everyday business life and are living a more free and easy-going life on your boat.

There are, however, many established boat yards around the country where you may find temporary employment for your skills. It is even possible to find a local guy building his own boat who would employ an extra person when the job requires two sets of hands.

Working for a while for a local boat yard can really supplement your cruising kitty, and as I said before, boat yards, especially if they build boats as well as repair them, employ people of many different skills. The larger yards are almost always looking for skilled employees. Even unskilled work is usually available: sanding and grinding boat bottoms, sanding and prepping paintwork, and masking up before spray painting is started. Even sweeping up around the yard is a necessary job that doesn't tax you too much.

Working for a boat yard does not necessitate your having to buy a lot of equipment; when you are ready to move on, there is nothing tying you down. You can build up your cash and then go cruising for a while longer.

Many, many boats of every style and size have been built from the keel up by ordinary people, who accomplished this with just a lot of common sense, a set of plans, a little money for the materials to get started, and a lot of hard work. They saved money each week and each month, buying more materials as the craft took shape, and with a dream and perseverance, one day the launch date arrived. You can do the same. When you see your owner-built boat floating on the water, you will be higher than a kite, without the need of alcohol or drugs.

There are countless books on the subject of boat building, covering every type of construction, whether you intend to build in ferrocement, fiberglass, wood, steel, or aluminum. You can read how to build from blueprint plans and how to loft the lines from the table of offsets, supplied by the designer. You may read details of construction that you don't understand, but if you read them again and again the meaning will often come to you, and you will understand exactly what you need to do. If you are still puzzled, you can always find an experienced boatwright who will do your lofting for a few hundred dollars. Often someone working in a local boatyard will be glad to work with you, to earn some extra pocket money for night or weekend work.

One does not have to be a highly skilled craftsman, though this would speed the process. You can learn as you go: Some colleges and high schools have classes in shop, woodworking, metal shop, machining, and so forth.

Also, when you get started on a project of this size, you will find that different people will be coming around to watch the progress. You will be surprised how helpful people can be, both physically and with advice as to how this or that is built. Many retirees, with a world of experience and various skills, just love to see a project like yours take shape. Having built four different boats in my life, I was always amazed and pleasantly surprised at how helpful neighbors were.

Sometimes "helpers" come to see you and just want to talk, which is great, but you can't spend all your time talking and visiting. Put a tool in their hands, and show them what you would like help with. The real helpers will stay, and the strictly "talkers" will soon leave. This I learned from an old boat-builder, but I'm afraid I did not always follow his advice.

Creating or building anything gives you a wonderful sense of accomplishment. Imagine what great feelings you will continue to have as your project grows and takes shape. The end result will be a source of great pride, not to mention the fact that the memory of the first time you went sailing in a craft you built with your own hands, will live with you for the rest of your life.

You will not regret the countless hours you spent building your dreamboat; almost as important, you will know every square inch of her. You will know where every single thing is located, every valve and fitting. If you have to find your way around her in the dark of night when you go cruising, this knowledge will give you a very secure feeling.

When or if things go wrong, it always happens when it is pitch dark or the seas have turned nasty with the wind howling. In your owner-built boat there will be much less chance of panic, since you will know exactly what to do.

A few boat builders I have known claim that they enjoyed building their boat as much as they did cruising, the feeling of accomplishment was so tremendous. When others say to you, "You are so lucky to have a boat and go cruising," you can reply, "Luck had little to do with it, just a lot of hard work, but it was really worth it!"

WHAT BOAT TO BUILD?

This is a subject that needs serious analyzing. What are your long-range plans? Are you going to use your boat for simple, short, day sailing? Are you more interested in fishing? Or just puttering around close to your home base? Do you want to go farther for overnight stays or weeks at a time? Have you dreamed of sailing off to a tropical island? For twenty years I had been dreaming about sailing to Tahiti; I finally sailed into Papeete harbor in 1973.

How large a boat do you want or need? How many people do you want to take with you? Are they family or friends? Some boats are designed to sleep eight or ten people, even more, yet have little or no storage for food and can barely carry enough supplies to last a couple of days. Besides, how many people do you know that you want to be in confined quarters with for an extended period of time?

A boat should have the minimum number of berths that you will need for your most crowded weekend sail. Too many berths take up valuable space which could be put to better use as storage areas for food and gear, especially if you plan a long ocean voyage. For this type of cruising you will need to carry every single thing you need for living. There are no stores on the ocean, so you need to make lists of essentials; where to store all these things is always a challenge.

What Material To Use To Build Your Dream Boat

Twenty or thirty years ago a great many boats were built of ferrocement, which was thought to be the answer to most of the problems boats suffer from: rust, marine borers or worms, blisters, and rot. These boats could also be built with relatively few tools. The framework was usually pipe, bent around into the shape of the hull. Tied to this were rods of steel running longitudinally or lengthways, over which were tied five or six layers of chicken wire or wire mesh: two layers inside the hull, and four or five layers on the outside.

With the complete hull, looking like a giant birdcage, all tied together tightly, a work crew was then needed for a day to cement the complete hull. The cement was laid on to the outside of the hull and squeezed through the mesh, so as to leave no voids in the hull. As the cement was coming through the mesh, part of the crew smoothed the inside of the hull, making it as fair as possible. Cement was not plastered on from both sides, as this would make cavities all through the mesh, which would cause rusting of the steelwork and blistering problems later.

If you are considering building a ferrocement boat, it is important to have a large enough crew so that the entire hull is completed in one day, with all the cement applied in one operation. Starting and stopping, doing the hull piecemeal, will create weak parts in the hull. When all cement work is completed, the whole structure must be covered with sackcloth or similar material, and kept damp with a water sprinkler or fogging system, spraying just the finest mist over the entire hull for a number of days, until the cement is completely cured. This can take a week or more, depending on the hull thickness and size.

When the hull is completed, about 20 or 25 percent of the finished boat is now done, perhaps less if you are fanatical about a beautiful finish, with handcrafted woods and exotic finishing of everything visible. Some fine yachts have been completed in three and four years, from start to finish, yet I have seen a beautiful wood schooner, a work of art, which took over twenty-five years to complete. Unfortunately, by then the owner was too old to realize his dream of going cruising.

But we were talking about cement boats.

Though, over the years, there have been many well built and beautiful ferrocement boats built, which have cruised successfully around the oceans of the world, there were many poorly built cement hulls. These created a problem for insurance companies; many of them cracked and sank, so it became very difficult, if at all possible, to obtain insurance on a cement hull. It is disappointing to have a sizeable investment that you cannot get covered by insurance.

I delivered a beautiful ferrocement 46-foot ketch to Auckland, New Zealand. We had found only one company in the U.S. that would insure the boat, but by the time we reached Auckland, the insurance company notified us that they were no longer insuring any ferrocement boats for cruising, and when our policy ran out, we were no longer insured. I might add that this particular ketch had been professionally built in New Zealand over twenty years earlier and had successfully crossed the Pacific quite a few times, spending different years cruising the islands of the South Pacific.

Of course, lots of people in small boats cruise the world without the umbrella of insurance coverage. Insurance becomes very expensive when you venture offshore, especially if the captain has not done the trip previously.

WOODEN BOATS

Wood boats have been built for centuries and are still being built today. This construction, however, requires a highly skilled craftsman to complete. Sailing craft are subject to tremendous pressures and strains, certainly on the high seas. When the ocean waves are kicked up by high winds, the forces upon a yacht become unbelievable. Wooden hulls tend to work and move more than other types of construction, so if a wood hull is not built very carefully, with every plank and frame fitted and fastened securely, it may leak—or worse, spring a plank, which might even cause a sinking.

Another problem is obtaining good straight lumber nowadays. This is partly because of the quick kiln-drying methods employed today in curing lumber. In the past, wood was left to dry in the air for long periods of time, which kept the wood straighter with fewer tendencies to warp. Today's lumber, even if fairly straight when you start, will often warp and twist when you run it through a saw. A plank with a nice fair curve may be just what you need in a certain place in the hull, but bent and twisted planks will give lots of headaches to a boatwright. Moreover, in today's world it is sometimes difficult if not impossible to locate certain fastenings for wood hull construction.

A beautiful, graceful, fair wooden yacht is a thing of beauty, and some purists would have nothing else, but all in all, building in wood is a difficult proposition and not to be undertaken lightly. Even these skills can be learned, but with great difficulty and much time.

FIBERGLASS CONSTRUCTION

The majority of boats built today are of fiberglass construction; most manufacturers use moulds, which make for speed and ease. Manufacturers can pop fiberglass boats out of the same mould, again and again, by the dozens or hundreds. But a free-lance builder, unless he has secured a mould (which is difficult), has to build an elaborate framework first. Over this framework the builder must start laying glass cloth impregnated with epoxy resin. Then the builder continues laying layer upon layer until the proper hull thickness is achieved, with much sanding and scratching done between layers, to make sure of a good bond.

The materials, also, dictate that the builder have knowledge of these chemicals and plastics, so you must read carefully the instructions for application and follow them implicitly. For environmental reasons our government has imposed restrictions and very strict regulations governing what chemicals or resins may be used. Some of the legal resins do not adhere to the under layer as well as others.

There is also the sanding dust to contend with, which necessitates the use of a dust mask, and the fumes given off by the resins require a real respirator.

Great care must be taken to squeeze out every air bubble as you resin the glass cloth. Any voids in the lay-up will eventually create problem blisters, which can be very expensive to repair. This problem may not appear for years, but blisters are sometimes very difficult to cure completely.

A well-built fiberglass hull is indeed fairly trouble-free, regarding maintenance, but it is doubtful if you can save any money by building one for yourself without a mould. Manufacturers will be hard to compete with. If you are set on a fiberglass boat, you may be able to buy the manufactured hull and finish the rest of the construction yourself. (Building in the furniture, etc., still requires glassing everything into the inside of the hull.) I have seen a few builders who acquired an unfinished hull and finished a fine yacht.

ALUMINUM CONSTRUCTION

Metal boats are, in my opinion, much easier to construct, if only for the simple reason that if you cut a piece of material too short, you can simply weld on the necessary similar material you need, and continue with your work. This type of construction will necessitate your learning to weld, and welding aluminum requires a more sophisticated welding machine than you can get by with when you are building a steel boat.

The latest aluminum welding machines are extremely sophisticated: They will pulse during welding, creating a beautiful ribbed weld. This makes the weld as perfect as if a machine or robot had done the weld. Also, the new type welder is so improved that it welds the material even if the pieces are not cleaned just perfectly.

Aluminum can be easily cut with a heavy-duty skill saw using a carbide blade, though cutting with the skill saw will send little sharp chips of aluminum flying every which way. To prevent sharp chips of aluminum getting into your eyes and to forestall a trip to the doctor's office, it is absolutely necessary to wear a full face shield and a pair of safety glasses or goggles. Welding aluminum necessitates that the metal be cleaned spotlessly, with no contamination left on the area to be welded, even in the cracks and joints. This cleaning takes much time and effort.

Aluminum must not be painted with anti-fouling paints, which contain copper or other metals. Two or three covering or sealing coats of a non-metallic primer must be used to insulate the aluminum from any paints that might have metallic ingredients in them.

There are many different grades of aluminum. The suppliers will tell you which material to use for a certain application.

Aluminum is a wonderful material for a racing boat, and many successful yachts have been built of this alloy, but in actual fact, aluminum and the salt-water environment do not go well together. First is the problem of electrolysis. Dissimilar metals immersed in an electrolyte create electrolysis. Salt water is an electrolyte. When two different metals are together in salt water, the more pure or more noble metal will make the less noble metal disappear into the water.

Second, the alloy used in the hull must be welded with welding wire or rod that is composed of the exact same alloy. All aluminum alloys look the same to everyone except to experts, who work with this material constantly, but you will see lettering and numbers on most aluminum, which will tell what alloy it is. (If it is brittle, it will crack if bent too much; if it is more pliable, it will be easier to bend and work.)

Electrolysis and alloy incompatibility can lead to serious problems. During a visit to Tahiti in 1984, I met the crew of a yacht that had just been hauled out for normal bottom cleaning and painting. The 50-foot aluminum yacht was only eight months old and had recently arrived in Papeete on a round-the-world cruise. However, when the crew was cleaning the bottom in preparation for painting, they noticed corrosion around the two recesses in the hull that housed the two drop-keels. (The drop-keels could be lowered down to improve the yacht's upwind sailing capabilities.)

The problem was that the keel boxes had been welded into the hull with a different alloy welding rod. The seams all around the hull recesses were almost devoid of welding. Electrolysis had eaten the welding away.

The crew of the French boat was then forced to remove much of the interior furnishings, to allow the hull to be rewelded without setting the interior materials on fire. This meant that a two- or three-day haul-out was now expected to last for months. This kind of tragedy could completely destroy the cruising funds, and though the owner appeared fairly wealthy, I'm sure he worried about other possible problems that might surface in the future.

There are, of course, many, many boats built of aluminum that have been very successful. I'm sure any serious racers would prefer the lightest, most affordable material possible, to give them every advantage in competition. A Frenchman in Tahiti, on a beautiful fiberglass yacht, said that he was going to have his next boat made of aluminum: This would make it possible to carry tons more girls! He then got married, which put a damper on that idea.

STEEL CONSTRUCTION

This, in my opinion, is the best material for any cruising sailboat in the over 30-foot size, though I have seen 30-footers built that worked out well. The thinner sheet steel used on a smaller hull is harder to work, making it more difficult to make a smooth, fair shell, unless the builder is a highly skilled metalworker.

The heat needed to weld the hull plating to the framing and the seam welding will cause buckling of the plating, even if the builder is careful and stitch-welds the hull—this is welding just a few inches, then moving to another area and welding another few inches, until the whole is welded. This helps to keep heat to a minimum, causing less warping. Much more care has to be taken when the material is eighth-inch thick or thinner. Of course, any builder wants his boat to look as fair and smooth as possible.

It may sound very difficult to a novice who has not had a lot of experience working with metal, but I have known four men who built their own sailing yachts in steel: a dentist, who constructed a 50-foot ketch; a chemical engineer, who built a 40-foot cutter; an architect, who built a 53-foot ketch; and a company manager, who built a 42-foot schooner. None of these brave souls was experienced in steel construction before they started to build.

It is essential to learn to weld, so you need to attend a course in welding, or have someone who is experienced teach you. You also must learn how to light an oxygen/acetylene cutting torch. This is what you will use to cut up the steel, whether it is the framing or the sheet steel, for plating.

Steel cutting can be easily learned with just a little practice. You can do this on remnants of scrap steel, which you can purchase inexpensively from a local scrap yard. Very soon you will be proficient at cutting it cleanly, and if you can't hold the torch steady, you can rest it against a heavy flat bar or angle iron. This you use as a guide, by laying it on the metal to be cut.

There are also cutting tips, called "drag tips." One allows you to cut metal by dragging the tip across the face of the metal. This keeps your hand and torch steady as you cut.

You will also need to practice welding, and this can be accomplished by welding together the different pieces of scrap metal that you just cut up. Just be sure not to buy scrap metal that has old paint or galvanizing on it, as this makes it very difficult to either cut or weld.

You do not need to become a certified welder to build your boat. It is always fairly easy to find a professional welder who would like to make extra money working nights or weekends, especially for cash. He will usually work for a reasonable rate. You can do all the fabrication and tacking things together, then have the experienced craftsman weld all the important seams.

There are many retirees everywhere, with all kinds of skills, who may be delighted to get involved in your project. Many people dream of building a boat and sailing off into the sunset, and helping you build your boat may be the closest they will ever come to doing it.

To build a traditional wineglass shape hull out of steel will take tremendous skill; however, a "hard chine" design is much, much simpler. Heavy-duty hard-chine hulls have been proven to sail almost as well as the wineglass shape hull. Some experienced sailors feel that the chine adds extra stiffness to a hull, which certainly helps in a heavy blow.

Both ketches that I built for myself were 48 feet on deck, 59 feet overall; both were hard chine construction, and both sailed remarkably well. When I was building them I bought 18-inch diameter steel pipe, which I split up into tapered sections. I welded these along the chine after rounding the framing at the chine to the same diameter as the 18-inch pipe. This made a much softer chine and also made it easier to plate the bottom and sides.

Actually the deck is laid on the framing first, and tacked in place. This stiffens the entire framing. Next the chine plates are fitted along each side, then the hull sides and transom, leaving the bottom plating to the last. This means that all the trash and used welding rods etc., fall out of the hull as work progresses, which saves a lot of clean-up time.

It has always been a concern to people that rusting will be a nightmare with a steel hull, and this could be a problem if the proper procedures were not followed. When the entire welding is completed, with all the welds ground smooth and any hull imperfections ground off—making sure that port holes, or any other fittings, have the necessary holes cut in—the entire outside of the hull must be sand-blasted. This means that every square inch of steel is blasted clean and white, then painted with epoxy primer.

To prevent any dampness getting into the pores of the steel, the blasting must be stopped early in the afternoon, the hull must be blown clean with compressed air, and the primer must be applied before the sun goes down. After sundown, the temperature falls below the dewpoint, and things get damp. If the sand blasting is done properly, and the entire hull is coated with two or three heavy coats of epoxy primer followed by a number of epoxy finish coats, the yacht will look great, and last for up to ten years or more.

If you damage the finish of a steel hull in any way, it is imperative that you touch up the blemish immediately, especially if the damage took the paint off down to the bare metal. This will ensure that rust does not even get a chance to start.

I have owned two steel ketches for more than ten years each, cruising them extensively, and never have had any serious problems with rust. Each time the boats were hauled for bottom painting, the task never lasted more than three days, with no rust or blister headaches to contend with.

The major benefit of a steel hull is its tremendous strength. Island-hopping once in the Society Islands of French Polynesia, we sailed up to a marker post set in the coral to denote the inside of the outer reef. We headed left to leave the marker to starboard, and at seven knots under sail, we ran hard up onto the reef. The hull was leaning over at about a twenty-degree angle, and we were aground hard and fast. (Later, when I re-read the sailing instructions for that area, I saw that it noted that care should be taken with markers, since sometimes they are installed inverted by mistake, with the triangle point up instead of down, or vice versa.)

We immediately dropped the genoa and mainsail and started the 120-horsepower diesel engine, trying again and again with full throttle in reverse to back off, but she would not budge. The trade wind was still blowing the normal eighteen to twenty knots, and it was sickening to feel the hull crunch against the coral, with the wind gusts pushing the masts over and back—though, ever so little, the hull was moving and making a bed for itself in the coral. I wondered what damage the hull was suffering.

I checked below, raising the engine room hatch, and was happy to see that no water was running into the bilge, which collects any water coming into the boat if there is a leak any place in the hull. We were about to move any heavy gear as far aft as possible, and maybe fill with water the dinghy hanging on davits across the stern. These things would lower the stern and hopefully raise the bow, which was the only part of the hull stuck on the coral.

Then my first mate said, "Just try it one more time with the engine," which I did, backing down as hard as the engine would pull. After a few minutes, ever so slowly, the boat started to inch back. Apparently the hull movement had crunched the coral down enough, and we eased off, to my great relief.

I had been worrying about what to do if we couldn't free her from the coral. There is little tidal difference in the Tahiti area, to help with a high tide. Just what would it cost to have a tugboat come all the way over from Papeete? Our cruising budget would have been kaput, finito, gone.

We immediately motored around the other side of the marker and into the first little bay to anchor. I put on a facemask and flippers and went over the side to view the damage. We had run hard aground, and ground and crunched on coral for over an hour. Yet I was amazed to see no dents or damage at all. Only the bottom paint was scraped off over a large area, down to the epoxy primer, which was mostly still intact. I had heard and read stories of steel boats being up on the rocks, sometimes for days, and being pulled off again, the hull still water-tight, and I was sure glad I had a steel hull under me when I was high and dry on the coral. For a cruising boat, steel is hard to beat.

Steel hulls also make it very simple to have built-in fuel tanks. The whole forward section can be made into two large tanks, which in my 48-foot ketch held a total of 1,000 gallons of diesel. This also made the forward part of the hull double skin, as it were, which may have saved her from sinking in the event of holing the under-body forward--we may have lost diesel fuel, but we would have stayed afloat. It also takes care of all that space under the flooring, which is hard to paint and service.

Carrying all that fuel down low is good ballast; it also means you don't have to get questionable or dirty fuel out of drums in every little island you visit. Fueling is difficult in many places, if not impossible.

There is no doubt that building a boat is an enormous undertaking, not only in the amount of labor that needs to be performed, but also in the continuous saving and spending of money, month by month, for materials as you progress. You are actually building a complete, self-contained home that must be able to withstand being knocked down and slammed about on a stormy sea, yet be able to stay together in one piece and bring you safely to your destination.

The length of time it takes to build from start to finish varies a great deal, depending upon size, complexity of design, and finish. Other factors are the skill of the builder, how much money is available, how much time the builder can devote to the project, if friends are available to help, and if one can afford to employ, at times, some outside skilled labor or subcontractors.

My first 48-foot ketch took three and a half years to complete, working two nights every week and every Saturday, all day. Any holidays or vacations were also spent working on my dreamboat. Then the second ketch, started ten years later, took five years to complete, though it was similar in size. I spent more time the second time, finishing off with much more teak and stainless steel.

I have known a few builders who enjoyed the building so much that they extended the work for twenty years and more. On the other hand, I met an attorney from the Los Angeles area who had built a large ferrocement yacht in twelve months. He related the story of how he had big KFC feeds every Saturday, with lots of people coming around to help. He would hold up a piece of equipment and say, "OK, who wants to install this?"

Unfortunately, after cruising through French Polynesia and on to the Cook Islands, while cruising around the Rarotonga area he was coming back into port at night, misjudged the entrance, and ran hard aground. The damaged hull filled with water and sank, falling off the reef and settling on the bottom in very deep water. Everything was lost.

I met him shortly after this disaster, but he was very upbeat, saying he was going to start building another similar yacht immediately. He laughed, "Well, the last boat had a lot of things that did not work, so this time, I'm going to take more time to build it—maybe thirteen months."

I can't imagine completing a boat in such a short time, but with enough money and a big group of helpers, who knows?

Whichever way you do it, the experience of constructing your own cruising yacht will be a very rewarding one that will give you good feelings and memories for the rest of your life. The accomplishment will certainly satisfy your creative urge, and when someone says in disbelief, "You built this?" you will swell with pride.

You can also sail away from it all, and go any place in the world you desire, without a ship's captain or airline pilot taking you there.

You will be free as the wind.

CRUISING TO DISTANT PORTS   5

Most of my life I have enjoyed reading books about the sea. I pored over Jack London's novels, most of them really about his own experiences as a regular seaman. Around twelve years old, I devoured the story *Robinson Crusoe* by Daniel De Foe. Later, *Swiss Family Robinson* also intrigued me because of the last name, which was my own.

When I read of the sailing experiences of Joshua Slocum—I believe the first solo around-the-world sailor, aboard *Spray*, a 36-foot shallow-draft hull with a remarkable 14-foot beam—I was getting ideas about going to distant ports.

Could it really be possible?

Sir Francis Chichester, the noted English yachtsman, who started an exciting life as a seaplane pilot, flying solo around the world, later in life took up sailing, accomplishing remarkable feats. His many sailing exploits he wrote about with great skill.

I also found the very informative books by Eric and Susan Hiscock, who had sailed around the world many times, writing in detail of their experiences. Eric's book *Cruising Under Sail* is thought by many sailors to be one of the best books ever written on the subject. Eric was an excellent author and photographer with a world of knowledge; his books are easily read and full of important information.

I was fortunate to meet up with Eric and Susan Hiscock in French Polynesia two different times, the last one in Bora Bora in 1984. They were both in their late seventies and though living in New Zealand, had decided to sail up to Bora Bora one more time. Some "sail"—it was probably about 4,000 miles each way. We had lunch together. They were a delight to visit with, and their books are well worth hunting down.

When I was young I never dreamed it would be possible to someday sail to faraway places. However, as the years passed and I read more and more of other people's experiences, I started to wonder, why not? I made a ten-year plan, promising myself to have a boat by then and take a year off work and go cruising.

With that dream in mind, I started to work toward that end. I looked at many boats for sale, and each time, the ones in my price range were in need of major refitting. I eventually felt I might do as well to build one from scratch.

It took a lot of dedication and hard work, but eleven years later I had the 48-foot steel ketch *Seahorse* finished and sailing for a few years. All my bills were paid up for a year; the tanks were full of diesel and water, and there were provisions aboard for four people for a year. We would buy fresh bread, vegetables, and fruit on the way; we were ready to head south.

Even when the boat is complete, the crew must sail her a lot and practice everything: sail-changing, handling the boat under sail and power, engine operation and maneuvering, and time and time again, the "man overboard" drill. This is extremely important; each crew person should be skilled at bringing the boat back to a certain spot.

We would pick a helmsperson; I would throw a buoyant cushion overboard and yell, "Man overboard." It was then the helmsperson's job to give orders. One person had to stand up forward, in the helmsperson's view, and do nothing but point toward the "person/ cushion" in the water, never taking his eyes off the cushion for a second, no matter what the boat or crew was doing.

The rest of the crew got the engine started and the sails down. The helmsperson wheeled the boat around, watching the person pointing, and followed their directions. The yacht could be wheeled around before the sails came down, but they should be doused as quickly as possible.

In the past, even very experienced sailors have not been able to stop close by the person in the water, but have sailed right past, one, two, and three times, even eventually losing the person to drowning. It is important to get the motor running and the sails down; then you can more easily put the boat exactly where you need to.

It is imperative that everyone on board learn this drill, because the captain may be the one overboard.

There are food lists to prepare and lists of necessities to make. This means just about everything, especially if you are going to be on the ocean for a month or more with four or five others.

How much bread can you use before it starts to mildew and grow mold? Can you make bread on the way? How many eggs do you want to take? How will you store them? (We found that buying eggs in the plastic or Styrofoam cartons instead of cardboard, coating each egg with Vaseline, and just storing them in a locker would keep them fine for many weeks. The Vaseline covering the pores of the eggshells helps to keep them without refrigeration.)

If you are blessed with a good sea cook, you are indeed lucky, as this is the most difficult job on the boat when on the ocean. A good cook will organize the whole galley and oversee the stocking of all your supplies—including finding out what each crewmember likes or hates to eat, and provisioning accordingly.

If you don't have a cook willing to prepare all the meals, you must designate, and rotate different crewmembers to cook. You may find one really good at breakfasts and another who will prepare dinner. Then you can schedule their watches to be during the breakfast or the dinner shift. The captain or another crew person can keep watch during the cooking of the meal.

Having the crew rotate as chef will occasionally produce a meal that is not quite what you had hoped for. However, it has been my experience that more often than not, the meal far exceeded my expectations. Some who claimed they could not cook at all, supplied the most delicious dishes.

Of course, the first few days on the ocean, no one wants to eat a lot, much less cook, until they get their sea legs. It is a very good idea to start off the trip with a large pot of rich, but not highly seasoned, soup or stew, which can be easily heated and reheated many times and is a great comfort to tender tummies, especially if the weather is cold.

Seasickness is a malady which most of us have to put up with, and being the expert that I am on the subject, I know just how one feels when seasick. I've tried just about everything I have ever heard of, but to no avail. Every time I go to sea after being on land for a long time, *mal de mer* rears its ugly head, and I can chum the waters like an expert. As yet I have not tried taking or chewing ginger, which some sailors swear by. Next time it is on the list.

Most people say, "Oh, I couldn't sail across an ocean, because I get seasick." But over the years I have asked hundreds of sailors, who are sailing the oceans of the world, about this subject. I gather from their comments that about 95 percent of them get seasick when they first go to sea. Some of the greatest sea captains of all time, including Admiral Lord Nelson and Captain James Cook, had the same problem. My friend and first mate Jozo was the only one I have sailed with who never showed the slightest sign of seasickness or discomfort on the ocean.

I was told by an old sea dog that seasickness is mostly caused by fear when the person loses sight of the land and is surrounded by water. However, I'm convinced that this is only in some rare cases. I am not apprehensive about being away from the land, after having sailed more than 25,000 ocean miles.

In fact, it is more worrisome when you start getting close to land. Close to land you can run aground or be run over by the more plentiful shipping, while at sea you only have to watch out for the occasional ship. Far from land you very seldom even see another ship.

At one time the charts showed the sailing routes of the world; because they showed favorable winds or currents, these charts were very important to sailing or low-powered ships. Crossing the ocean in the area marked as a sailing route was reason to keep a sharper lookout. However, nowadays, ships are more powerful and more plentiful. They crisscross the oceans of the world, going almost directly from port to port. Therefore, you might find one anywhere, and being run down by a large ship is the most dangerous thing you have to face, sailing offshore.

Big ships always have radar operating, even if the officer on watch is not looking at it constantly. You can make yourself relatively safe by installing a radar alert on your craft. The radar alert is an electronic device that will sound a warning in your cabin if a radar is operating in your area. When it beeps, you will know there is a ship out there someplace. Some radar alerts have a built-in compass or indicator that will show you the direction towards the ship. This helps you locate the ship that might be bearing down on your craft. Sometimes you will get a signal that a ship is in the area, yet it may never appear, being just over the horizon. At least you have been alerted.

A radar alert is a very important piece of equipment: No one should go to sea without one. Often radars today come with radar alerts built in, which is great, but sailboats usually do not have the battery capacity to operate the radar continually. A separate alert uses so little power it can be left on all the time.

In addition to the radar alert, you should have a good radar reflector up the mast or at the masthead; this will show your craft as a larger target or blip on the radar screen of the approaching ship.

Organizing a crew takes time and is sometimes very difficult. You hope to get experienced sailors who will all get along well with each other. However, it is not always possible for the ones you would like to come along to get the time off work or business. You usually have a limited choice, and often have to settle with inexperienced crew who may never have sailed on the ocean before, or even been sailing at all. A crew with no experience may work out just fine if they are of the right mind set, willing to help in any way and anxious to learn.

Even though it is wonderful to have a crew person who really knows his or her stuff, which takes a load off your shoulders, it is also disconcerting to have a semi-skilled crewmember second-guess your orders and argue about how you run your cruise. In my own experience, the three best crewmen have been three guys on different trips who had little or no previous experience on a sailboat, yet were anxious to learn and had a lot of common sense.

No Crew To Help?

There may be times when it is impossible to find crew. Therefore, the boat should be set up for single-handed sailing, meaning the boat can be handled by one person. This can be done even with larger boats of 60 to 75 feet and even up to mega-yachts.

In fact, while anchored in Fiji, I watched a 150-foot yacht get under way. One man was on the foredeck, stepping on the anchor windlass button. The anchor came up and self stowed, at which point the skipper up in the midships cockpit pressed buttons and worked levers. One by one the sails unfurled and set themselves, and the yacht sailed noiselessly away. I'm sure the skipper had an anchor windlass control button on his console, and could have done the whole departure himself.

To set up for single-handing, you absolutely need a heavy-duty autopilot, one with a power unit to move the rudder of a boat half again as big as your boat. This will assure that even in heavy weather, your pilot will not be straining at the top of its capabilities but can easily handle the strain hour after hour without failing. Spares for the autopilot should also be carried.

Even if you know nothing about electronics, it is amazing what a person can do with a good instruction manual. Many parts nowadays just plug in. Also if you have the new parts, you can often find someone who understands electronics and can get you going again. It is even possible to install two pilots independent of each other, and switch from one to the other. Then you always have a back-up system.

A wind vane system will hold a course for you based on the wind direction, though with the wind vane, you have to check your heading frequently. The wind veering around will affect the course the vane will steer, so if the wind comes around 180 degrees, your yacht will be taking you back to your starting point.

Whichever way you go, some means of self-steering is a must for a person sailing alone. It is fun to steer for a while, out day-sailing, but if you cannot balance your sail plan to have the boat sail herself on a desired course, you will be an exhausted zombie by the time you reach your destination.

With a crew of five on my last trip from San Francisco to Nuku Hiva in the Marquesas Islands, a distance of 3,200 miles, I asked each crew member how long they had actually steered *Seahorse 2* during their watches. Only one person had steered more than a few hours, and he had switched the pilot off during his watch occasionally, because he liked to steer. He felt it relieved the boredom of the night watches.

Roller reefing and furling is also a wonderful way to handle the sails, especially the headsails. Roller systems make it unnecessary for a crew person to work up on the plunging foredeck in rough weather.

At one time it was not prudent to have roller furling on a cruising boat, in case it got stuck or jammed half in and half out, with no way to get rid of it, maybe with a gale brewing. Roller furling systems, however, have been greatly improved over the years, and malfunctions nowadays are rare, especially if one does the suggested maintenance: washing out the roller system, etc., or lubricating if it is recommended.

I have never regretted installing roller furling. Among its benefits are the two sail slots, which allow you to fly two genoas at the same time when running downwind—just like a spinnaker, but more easily handled. When it comes time to shorten or get rid of sails, you simply roll the two sails up together, and they are gone in a few seconds.

I had an experience with an 1,800-square-foot spinnaker on *Seahorse* en route to Tahiti in 1973. We had talked about hauling up the spinnaker behind the mainsail, with the halyard around the winch a couple of turns. This worked fine the first few times we flew the spinnaker. Unfortunately, some days later my best crew man, Jozo, was hauling up the spinnaker without the halyard being around the winch, and just as the spinnaker almost reached the mast head, it popped out full of wind. Though Jozo tried to hold onto the halyard, it was impossible to check the pull of the filled sail.

I was up on the foredeck and noticed out of the corner of my eye that over the side, the spinnaker was skimming over the waves like a gigantic white sheet on the water. I glanced back at Jozo, who was still holding the halyard, but blood was seeping out from between all his fingers. It was a painful two or three weeks for Jozo, though with his both hands bandaged, he stood all his watches without a single complaint.

Spinnakers are wonderful if you have a large, experienced crew, but for safety's sake, they have no place on a cruising boat, certainly not when sailing with a small crew.

The mainsail may also be on a roller system. There are different designs on the market, some rolling the sail up inside the mast, or rolling up into a special aluminum housing fastened to the aft side of the mast. Other systems have the sail rolling down, inside the boom.

If the sail has full-length battens at the reef points, the boom stowing system would seem to be the ideal way to go. The battens would keep the foot of the sail straight, getting rid of the problem of the sail's puckering up and wrinkling badly, which is the main problem with roller furling/reefing systems in general. Wrinkled and baggy sails give you more problems, especially in high winds, which is just when you have to reef.

I have never used a system which rolls the sail into the mast; though the system looks good, it may be necessary to bring the bow up almost into the wind to help prevent the sail's wrinkling up too much.

With no roller system to help you shorten sail, the jiffy reefing system is the next best thing. This system is an improvement over the old-fashioned way of having to lower the sail; fasten the tack, or front end, and also the out-haul cringle at the back end of the sail; tie in all the reef lines along the boom; then haul the sail up tight again.

The jiffy reefing system has lines going from a fastening at the extreme forward end of the boom, up through the reefing cringle or hole, and back down to a fair lead on the mast at the level of the boom, down to a block leading it back to the cockpit. This will haul down the front part of the sail when you are ready to do so.

There is a similar line running from a fastening on the back end of the boom, aft of where the aft reefing cringle will be when the sail is reefed. From the boom fastening, the line goes up through the aft reefing cringle in the sail, then back down to a turning block on the side of the boom, which leads the line forward through two more turning blocks, taking it back to the cockpit. This line will control the back end of the sail when you are ready to reef.

The halyard is then eased down and both reefing lines are pulled in until the sail is down to the boom, stretched tight fore and aft. Then the halyard can be hauled up tight again. At this point, you have the sail reefed and under control, and it is not so difficult to tie in the reef point cringles, pulling the foot of the sail down against the boom.

There is also a simplified single-line reefing system, which has to be set up with double blocks, running back and forth inside the boom, as the following page illustrates. With this system, to reef the sail very simply you need only ease the halyard down as you crank in on the single line. I think this may be the best way to go, because of the simplicity of it. You can have the single reefing line leading back to a self-tailing winch in the cockpit.

It is important to have adequate-sized winches, large enough to handle the loads of heavy-weather sailing which will come your way sooner or later. The fact that your sails can be hauled in tight using a small winch cranked by a six-foot, six-inch, 250-pound teenager, is of no consequence, unless he is a permanent member of your crew.

Large, powerful winches are a great help in keeping fatigue at a minimum. When I was younger, I sailed for ten years on a 40-foot racing sloop which had no sheet winches at all. In any kind of blow, the bow of the boat had to be brought up almost into the wind to spill the wind out of the sails, allowing them to be sheeted in hard, by hand. The problem with this is that the slatting of the sails, before you can bear off and fill them again, is very hard on everything, especially the sails, as they bang and rub against the mast and standing rigging (the wires holding up the mast).

In sailing you have to pay continual attention to chafing, or wear, as sails or ropes rub against a wire, rope, spreader end, or lifeline. When chafing goes on hour after hour, or day after day, the stitching holding the sail panels together wears through, and the sail can start to come apart—more so when the wind freshens.

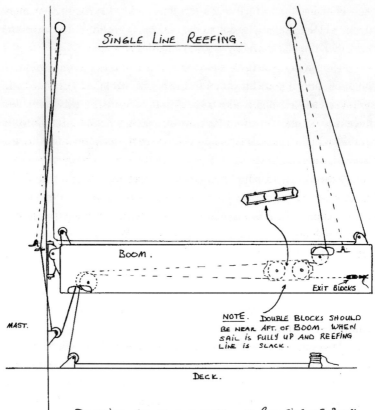

SINGLE LINE REEFING.

BOOM.

A

EXIT BLOCKS

NOTE. DOUBLE BLOCKS SHOULD BE NEAR AFT. OF BOOM. WHEN SAIL IS FULLY UP AND REEFING LINE IS SLACK.

MAST.

DECK.

DRAWING SHOWS ONE REEF. ON PORT SIDE OF BOOM. SECOND REEF LINES ARE FITTED ON STB. SIDE OF BOOM. SECOND REEF CANNOT BE HIGHER THAN THE LENGTH OF BOOM ALLOWS TRAVEL OF DOUBLE BLOCKS.

On my first boat, which had twin head stays, there was an almost new jib stowed on the port head stay, underneath the genoa we were using on the starboard stay. Parts of this jib were resting against the pennant holding down the tack of the genoa. There was obviously slight movement of the jib against the wire pennant—just a fraction of an inch, but over the period of three or four days, when we needed to hoist it, we found five large holes worn clean through the tack or front of the jib. It made me much more careful about chafe in the future.

This goes for ropes and lines where they go through turning blocks. You must ease the line or haul it in just a little to move the rope; then the block will be rubbing on a different place on the line.

When a line starts to show wear but is not yet frayed through the outer fibers, you can prolong its life by end-for-ending it, which simply means changing its ends around so that the end that was at the sail is now the end at the cockpit. This will now give you the same length of time to use it over. If you wait until the line is frayed through, the remainder of the line may not be long enough after you cut off the damaged part, but end-for-ending will almost double its life.

Anchoring gear is of the utmost importance. Having it simple to operate will make life much more enjoyable. You also need a heavy-duty windlass to do the work.

A few cruisers use a combination of nylon line with a short piece of chain at the anchor. If you have a long enough nylon line and enough swinging room to lie to a long anchor rode, you can get by with this system for a while.

However, this system has a couple of faults: First, when you are weighing the anchor and the line changes to chain, the rope wildcat does not handle chain well. It is sometimes very difficult to get the chain over to the chain gypsy, which is usually on the other side of the small windlass. It is also easy to get one's fingers caught between the windlass and the chain.

The second fault is chafe, which we spoke about before, but this time it can be taking place under water, where you can't even see it. If you are anchored in a rocky place or near coral, as you swing around with the wind or current, the line can be chewed through in short order. Even where the anchor line rests on the deck chock, or anchor roller, it may eventually wear through and weaken. All of the preceding makes it uncomfortable for you to leave your boat, even for a relatively short period of time.

On the other hand, most cruisers use all chain and a heavy anchor. The benefits far outweigh the cost of the gear.

All chain, of course, requires a strong windlass, either electric or hydraulic. The chain locker should be large and tall enough to have the chain completely self-stowing. If the chain locker is not tall enough, the chain builds up in a mound until it jams against the top of the locker and stops. It is then necessary for you or a crewmember, in the middle of weighing anchor, possibly with anchor just broken out, to rush down to the forward cabin, open the chain locker access panel, and flake out the chain.

The chain jamming in the pipe stops the whole operation. This can be a real nuisance, especially if you are in a hurry to weigh anchor or are single-handing. This scenario may even become disastrous if you've just gotten the anchor broken out.

The problem is compounded if you are in a tidal or windy area and the boat starts to move as the anchor breaks out. It is very difficult to simultaneously be on the foredeck, down in the forward cabin flaking out the chain, and also at the helm to control the yacht from drifting down on another boat or the beach. Even Houdini or Superman would be in trouble trying to perform this feat.

When you are deciding what windlass to buy, you have to figure the heaviest load it will be subjected to when you go cruising. Some anchorages will have depths of up to one hundred feet and more, which will necessitate laying out almost all of your chain. This is quite a load to pick up, more so if the wind is blowing. If you have 300 feet of chain out and the anchor weighs eighty to 100 pounds, with the wind blowing at twenty knots, a windlass with pulling power of 1,000 pounds will not be adequate. You will have to power the yacht up to the anchor, cinching up on the chain, and use the boat to break out the anchor, especially if you have been anchored for a time and the anchor is well dug in.

Some manufacturers are optimistic when they rate their windlasses, so it is best to buy one rated at three to four times the weight you will be picking up. A powerful windlass with a totally self-stowing chain is really important to a sailor cruising alone.

I had always wondered what it would be like to sail across an ocean alone. I had read so many articles written by the famous (and some not-so-famous) sailors, giving details of their feelings when at sea for long periods of time, alone—their concerns, the loneliness, the dangers, and the great joy and satisfaction at concluding the passage successfully.

At the end of a year-long cruise in French Polynesia, and now faced with the long trip back to San Francisco with no crew, the time seemed perfect to find out exactly what it would be like.

In Papeete harbor, November 15 dawned—another beautiful day in Paradise—as I weighed anchor, first hauling in on the buoyed nylon tripline I had tied to the head of the 100-pound CQR anchor, to assist in breaking it out. After being tied stern to the quay in Papeete for two and a half months, the anchor was really bedded in.

Papeete harbor is foul with many anchors and chains that have been discarded as unretrievable by yachtsmen who stayed too long at the quay. There is a very heavy hurricane cable stretched tightly along the bottom, parallel to the quay and approximately 150 feet out from the wall. This cable is there for anchors to hook onto if the anchor starts to drag. Ships and ferryboats coming and going create quite a surge, which happens all too often. Yachts start to pull and tug at their anchor cables, and unless they are well set with maximum scope, they will drag and eventually hook on the large bottom cable. Great care should be taken to put out as much scope as possible in Papeete; it is almost a necessity to use a trip line and marker buoy to assist you in breaking the anchor out when it comes time to leave, if you can finally tear yourself away.

Fueling was easily accomplished over by the ferryboat docks; the fuel is a little cheaper in Papeete than in the outer islands, since you save the extra shipping costs.

With my bond money returned to me, my twelve-gauge shotgun back on board (the authorities hold all firearms until you are about to leave), the water tanks full, and much food on board, I sailed out of Papeete harbor with a sad heart at leaving, but sadness mixed with excitement for the voyage ahead.

Seahorse 2 is a wonderfully fast steel ketch and though 59 feet overall, is very easily handled. The Benmar Cetrec automatic pilot had not once faltered during the four years since *Seahorse 2* was launched. I prayed the autopilot would continue to work as it had always done. I had found the Benmar pilot to be one of the best pieces of marine equipment I have ever run across. I had used the power unit recommended for an 85-foot fishing boat, and it worked tirelessly, with never a sound or complaint, even steering in a hurricane later.

With a southwest breeze of ten miles an hour, 130 miles had passed under the keel, when 12:00 noon the next day rolled around and I plotted the noon position. How nice it is to have a satellite navigation system and just press a button to get a fix. During my first cruise, there was only celestial navigation with the sextant and tables to guide a mariner. Only the U.S. Navy had satellite navigation systems. (Of course, there is a great deal of satisfaction in reaching your destination, having done it all by yourself.)

Day after day the trade winds held steady although light at around ten miles per hour, but *Seahorse 2* slipped right along with day runs of 127 to 150 miles when the breeze freshened to fifteen mph.

The first week passed fairly uneventfully, although the engine cooling water pump, which pulls water in from the sea through the engine, then into the exhaust to cool it, was not working properly. Even after changing the pump impeller, it still worked only intermittently. I could only run the engine for fifteen minutes at a time, every four or five hours. However, although it wouldn't drive the boat, this schedule kept the refrigerator cold, the freezer frozen, and the batteries charged.

On Saturday, eight days out of Papeete, I wrote in my log how well things were going. I had not been seasick on this trip, which was unusual for me. The sea was fairly calm, the light breeze steady, and since I had skipped lunch, I was hungry. It was now 5.30 P.M., so I prepared a tossed green salad with chopped onions, green peppers, and beets. This was followed by a New York steak, baked potato, fresh carrots, and French bread, and finished with coffee and two cookies.

I always had my coffee while sitting up on the bowsprit watching for dolphins, flying fish, or other sea life. When it got dark I went below and watched a video movie as a special treat, courtesy of my friends Mike and Dianne, who had thoughtfully brought a selection of movies when they visited us in Bora Bora. So...this single-handing is so tough?

The following Monday the weather turned squally and the wind suddenly changed direction a few times, causing the 150 percent genoa that I was flying at the time, to get caught around the spreader end and suffer a three-foot tear in the dacron. I had seen the America's Cup team tear a genoa, yet have another one flying again in a minute and a half.

However, I proved to be not so speedy: It took almost one and a half hours before I had the torn sail down and the replacement genoa up and set. Then I spent a day and a half hand-sewing the torn sail back together again. In the meantime, I had been using an almost new sail, so as soon as I had the old one repaired, I put it back on. (I prefer to use old sails for ocean crossings, since sails suffer from chafe; I like to keep a good suit of sails to use when in view of others or near land.)

During the night another squall hit fiercely. As *Seahorse* charged through the seas, she plunged her bow into a wave so hard that one of the teak boards on the bowsprit was smashed off, leaving a gaping hole just where you would step if walking out on the bowsprit. When I noticed the board was gone, I thought, *I must tie ropes across the slats to prevent me from falling through the hole.* But laziness is one of my problems, and I thought, *Oh, I'll remember that hole.*

The very next night at around 3 A.M. I was awakened by the squealing and splashing of a fantastic school of dolphin playing and leaping out of the water all around the boat, as we sailed along at seven knots. I always enjoy a visit from these most interesting creatures, which appear to have such a wonderful time. As I made my way up to the bow to watch them play in the bow wave, my left leg went down through the hole in the bowsprit, right up to my knee. But for the fact that I had one hand on the pulpit and the other hand on the headstay, with a firm grip, I would probably have broken my leg.

Although my leg was only badly bruised, I almost went into shock. I stood there realizing just how bad a situation I could have been in. I had very sobering thoughts of how stupid and careless I had been. What would I do hundreds of miles from land, by myself, with a broken leg?

I vowed to be more careful in the future.

Before this trip, I had been concerned that I would not be able to rest or sleep at all, that I would be constantly on watch for other shipping. However, as the days passed without a sign of any other living soul, I became more blasé. Instead of practicing my habit of getting up to look around every half hour or so, I would find myself lying in the aft cabin, reading a book and thinking, *Well, I haven't been up on deck for about three hours, so maybe I should go take a look.* This is really sloppy watchkeeping, and I never thought of myself as the reckless type. I did have the radar alert switched on, though.

Then two days later I was sitting up in the helmsman's seat reading, shortly after noon, and looking up because the radar alert was beeping. I saw a container ship on the horizon. As I continued to check on his position, I became concerned, since the bearing to the ship did not change, meaning that we were on a collision course.

It being a lot of trouble for me to come about and change course, I grabbed the radio mike and called on channel 16, which all shipping is supposed to monitor.

Three times I called and got no response, so I was just about to alter the autopilot course, when the radio crackled into life and the captain of the ship said I could hold my course. He altered his course, and passing ahead of my bow, cleared me by about one hundred yards. We then talked for a little, and the captain of the *Osaka Maru* very kindly sent a telegram to my family, giving my position and stating that everything was OK.

Afterwards I shuddered to think I may not have had a radar alert, and may have been in my bunk as the *Osaka Maru* bore down on me. I'm convinced they had not seen me, nor had they known I was even there until I called them on the radio.

That evening the wind piped up to around thirty-five knots, and with full sail including a 150 percent genoa, the *Seahorse* was flying right along at eight and nine knots. While I was lying in my aft cabin berth, from which the instrument panel is visible, I noticed the automatic bilge pump light on, indicating that it was pumping. Where was the water coming from?

I got up and upon examining the engine room bilge, I was startled to see water running along the engine bed stringer. Looking aft along the engine, I could see that the water appeared to be coming from the aft toilet. It being the middle of the night, I went back and closed both valves to the head and went back to bed.

After lying down, I glanced up at the panel and was upset to see the bilge pump light still on. I again opened the engine room hatch, and the water was still running into the bilge, only faster than ever. The lower pump was not keeping up with the water coming in; the water was now almost up to the top of the bilge. Now I was getting concerned. I noticed I was talking to myself as I crawled alongside the engine to try to find the problem.

Finally, I found that a stainless steel hose clamp had parted, and a one-and-a-half-inch hose was almost off the toilet holding tank. Although this holding tank had not been used and should have been empty, clear water was gushing out of the bottom of it. I just could not figure how this could be happening, since both valves to the head were closed, and the valve to the holding tank was also closed. Yet now I had about fifty gallons of water in the bilge, and it was rising.

It was only after struggling with the awkward job of fitting a new hose clamp, securing the hose, and stopping the flooding, that it dawned on me that the water must have been coming back into the waste tank through the tank vent hose. The vent hose through-hull is far above the water line normally, so it had never been fitted with a valve. Now that we were charging along between eight and nine knots, the stern wave was higher than the vent hose through-hull fitting, causing the filling of the tank and the flooding of the boat.

Lesson number umpteen thousand: Always have valves fitted on every hole in the hull, even those well above the water line. This I accomplished shortly after returning to land.

The remainder of the voyage was fairly uneventful. Seventeen days two hours, and two thousand seven hundred miles after leaving Papeete, I sailed into Hilo harbor in Hawaii and tied up, stern to the quay, in Radio Bay, by the U. S. Coast Guard station. I was elated that I had safely crossed an ocean by myself, but the miracle was that I had survived for seventeen days on my own cooking.

Alongside Radio Bay, the cruise ships tie up while they are in port. On my first night in port, I had gone to bed early, to get the first good night's sleep in almost three weeks. I was in a deep sleep when a blaring ship's horn brought me leaping out of the aft cabin berth. I grabbed the wheel and furiously turned it hard over, sure that I was being run down by a big ship.

When my eyes focused on my surroundings, I realized *Seahorse 2* was safely tied to the dock, and the cruise ship was leaving port, signaling with its horn. I had made the distance from being horizontal in the aft cabin to standing at the helm in one leap, I think, and was very relieved to find it was only a false alarm.

I had always held single-hand sailors in awe, but now I had just proven that any dummy could do it.

NAVIGATION AT SEA 6

Not too long ago, navigation at sea was a skill that took time to learn. Here is how to take a sextant sight, which measures the angle of the sun, moon, or star, above the horizon: Through a mirror fastened on the sliding arm of the sextant, you adjust the arm until the reflected image of the sun or other body is resting exactly on the horizon. Then read the degrees, minutes, and seconds of arc, which describe how far the body is above the horizon. At the same time, note the exact Greenwich mean time (which all navigation tables use) when the celestial body is right on the horizon.

Go into the logarithm tables, worked out years ago by mathematicians, using an assumed position; you will end up with a line of position, which is either toward or away from the assumed position. Put this line of position on your chart or plotting sheet.

A few hours later, do the same thing again, getting a new line of position, which you plot on your plotting sheet. Then move the earlier line of position along your course line the number of miles you have traveled since the earlier position. Now you have a running fix.

When you first start to use celestial navigation it takes anywhere up to two hours—sometimes longer—to get a line of position as you struggle through the steps, checking and rechecking your figures. However, as your skills improve, you will end up getting a line of position in about ten to fifteen minutes.

A U.S. Navy captain once told me to take three sextant sights, one right after the other, and work the three sights at the same time. If you have made a mistake in one, the others will show up the problem immediately. I started to do this, and occasionally it would show me a mistake before I plotted the line on the plotting sheet.

Before I set off for my first ocean crossing, San Francisco to Nuku Hiva in the Marquesas Islands of French Polynesia, 3250 miles distant, I had taken celestial navigation classes and felt that I understood the principle. I had, however, never taken a sight with an actual sextant. I had attended classes on celestial navigation, but all the altitudes of the sun and moon and star sights were given to us by the instructor of the classes.

After a few days of seasickness, with the *Seahorse* just heading on a course of 180 degrees due south, I started to take sights, one around eight o clock in the morning, then at noon, and again around four P.M. I would then mark our position on the ocean chart, on which I had drawn our great circle course line from San Francisco to Nuku Hiva. We seemed to be heading in the right direction, though occasionally we were a few miles off our course line. When that happened, we altered course a few degrees for a day, then went back on 180 degrees.

So we progressed, day after day, almost always on a course of 180 degrees, for twenty-two days, seeing only one other ship, which we tried to contact by radio to check our position, but to no avail. He never answered our calls; consequently, I was a little concerned about my figuring, and during the twenty-third day I said to Jozo, who had the early watch, that at first light the island of Nuku Hiva should be very visible, because it had very high mountainous peaks. Besides, we should be almost there.

I had trouble sleeping that night, getting up a few times to stand on the bowsprit, peering into the darkness hoping to see a light. I eventually went back to bed and fell into a deep sleep.

When I awakened at seven A.M. I looked back from the forward cabin to see Jozo, who was steering unconcerned, and I almost panicked. Jozo had not called me with the news of the island ahead. If it was not where I had calculated it to be, where was it?

I had four other human beings depending on me to find the island—*So, now do we steer north, south, east or west?* I could barely get my clothes on. I was shaking, and just didn't know what to say to the crew.

I hurried up through the main cabin, past the boys asleep and up into the cockpit. As I looked around, there was a big green island right off our starboard beam. We were sailing alongside of it.

I immediately looked at Jozo, and he started to laugh his head off, saying, "You should have seen your face while you were dressing; you looked like you were about to have a heart attack." Jozo had seen the mountains at first light but thought it might be fun to see my reaction.

He may have taken a few years off my life. I still recall the sick feeling I had in my stomach.

Each time thereafter, the islands appeared when and where they were supposed to be. It gives you a wonderful feeling when you have found your way successfully from place to place just with the sextant, chronometer, and tables.

Well, nowadays GPS global positioning systems have made navigation extremely simple and much more accurate than sights taken with the sextant while standing on a rolling, lifting, and falling deck. Since the advent of satellite navigation, even the positions of lots of islands have been corrected; some were miles away from the latitude and longitude at which they were plotted on older charts.

Navigation systems get better day by day, as technology increases and computers become more powerful. When I asked the price of satellite navigation sets prior to my 1973 cruise, I was informed that only the Navy had them. They were around $58,000.00 and were so large they would fill a small room. Since then they have been dramatically improved, and the price has dropped to where a handheld GPS, giving dozens of functions, costs a mere couple of hundred dollars.

I know of a couple who cruised the entire Pacific with only two small GPS handheld sets, one of which they kept wrapped up in plastic, stashed in a drawer, in case the one they were using gave up the ghost. They would then bring out the spare and continue on.

GPS not only gives you your position, but also supplies so many other functions. When you program in the latitude and longitude of your intended destination, you will be shown the bearing to your destination, the course to steer to get there, the speed you are traveling at, the length of time it will take you to get there, and the date and time you will arrive there if you continue at your present speed. The GPS also allows you to program in waypoints along your course, and will show you when you are closest to the waypoints.

These waypoints are extremely useful. They enable you to have your course plotted before you even leave the harbor. As well as spotting a course across an entire ocean, you can have a waypoint five miles this side of a small island, then a waypoint at the mouth of the harbor, another one halfway up a channel, and one at a particular spot in a large anchorage where you intend to anchor. It could not be much simpler to navigate your way into a strange harbor, especially if you also have a radar coupled to the GPS. This shows you the course line you are steering, with a ring around the spot you have made as a waypoint.

Now, I understand, there is a handheld global communications system that will also have navigation capabilities as well as acting as a fax machine and an E-mail system. This system will soon have voice capabilities allowing you to communicate with anyone, anywhere in the entire world. Is the Dick Tracy watch/radio/telephone here yet? I wouldn't be at all surprised.

Another wonderful navigation system is the GPS plotter, into which you can insert a small chart plug-in cartridge. Covering a very large area, the chart comes up on the screen with your boat's position on the chart. Your boat's position moves, exactly showing your position relative to the surrounding seascape, moving on the screen as you progress on your course. Your boat's position moves over the chart and you can see exactly where you are in relation to everything around you. The charts have all the pertinent information: depths, wrecks, submerged obstructions, channels, buoys, and everything you need to know to make a safe passage.

This piece of equipment can enable you to find your way in the dark, though it does not show you any other boats or moving objects, so you have to have radar working also. Then you are relatively safe moving, even on a pitch-dark night.

Of course, it is much more prudent to heave to off a strange harbor until daylight, then go in with full visibility.

It is possible to couple the automatic pilot to the GPS and radar; then you can dial in the latitude and longitude of your destination, and the pilot will take you right there. Of course, the pilot cannot avoid any obstruction that may be in your path, so you still have to keep a look out.

However, it is really wonderful, the way the new electronics operate, making life at sea so much more enjoyable, so much safer than in times past. I am reminded of my first trip, when George and I were coming back to San Francisco from Hawaii.

We were approaching the California coast after four days of heavy cloud cover, with not even a single sight of the sun, the moon, or a star; in the four days, we had traveled almost six hundred miles. At around four P.M. in a blinding rainstorm, we sighted a light that blinked on every six seconds.

I had already checked the chart: The light on Mile Rock at the south end of the Golden Gate Bridge was listed as a six-second light. I was elated, and we sailed on hoping to see the bridge any second. The heavy rain made visibility only about a hundred yards at most. I was up on the bowsprit, straining to see ahead, wondering if we should turn back.

Suddenly dead ahead appeared a giant rock, and I yelled back to George, who was at the helm, "Hard about!"

He responded immediately, wheeling the bow around to starboard, and with a crashing jibe, we were making our way out to sea again. After sailing for about half an hour, we dropped all sails except the main, and hove to, making almost no headway. We didn't want to get too far away from the coast.

We were now slowly heading towards Japan.

I had no idea where we were, without any means of navigation except the depth sounder; when it showed the same depth for quite a long time, I felt we were over a bank out off Bodega Head. We headed more south and just drifted all night, occasionally surrounded by the lights of other boats, who were probably fishing, and so passed a very uneasy night.

With the dawn the rain had stopped, and there peeping through the mist was the welcome light of Point Reyes lighthouse. We hauled up all sail and headed towards the Golden Gate, which was not yet visible, but was passing over our heads a few hours later as George and I shared a small bottle of champagne.

George thanked me for the most wonderful experience of his life. Maybe he was a little giddy and happy to see the land, but he did appear to really enjoy the trip.

George just reveled in the beautiful things in life, no matter how simple: learning to do celestial navigation; catching a five-foot mahi-mahi; eating most of it and making a necklace out of its spinal column, which he had cleaned to snow-white bone; seeing the sunrise over the ocean and beautiful sunsets near the tropics––I'm sure he still has as many vivid memories of that trip as I do.

There are times sailing the oceans when you say to yourself, "What the heck am I doing out here, when I could be home in a comfortable house?" But there are times when it is so beautiful, you can hardly go to bed, when the ocean is deep blue-black and the phosphorescence is like a billion diamonds sparkling in the water. Your craft glides noiselessly along, making a bubbling stream of diamonds swirling away behind, or a school of dolphin comes playing around the boat, especially at night, as they streak through the water like torpedoes, leaving a stream of phosphorescence in the water as if they had a propeller spinning at their tail.

Against the few times when things are difficult and a challenge, there are countless hours of happiness, if not pure joy, when you are so close to nature, it is like a religious experience. The good memories stay with you as long as you live

P.S. I later notified the U.S. Coast Guard of the duplication of the six-second light at Bodega Head and also at Mile Rock off San Francisco, and was told it would be corrected immediately.

SAFETY EQUIPMENT   7

The U. S. Coast Guard requires the following equipment to be carried on a yacht:

- A personal flotation device for each person on board.
- Sound producing device, a horn; also a bell if the yacht is over twelve meters, (thirty-nine feet, four inches).
- Navigation lights and shapes.
- Fire extinguishers.
- Visual distress signal flares, Coast Guard approved, three for day use and three for night use. These must be dated and current. (In certain areas, signal equipment rules differ; exempt from some of these rules are recreational boats less than 16 feet long, and open sailboats less than 26 feet long, if they are without mechanical propulsion.
- Manually propelled boats.
- Non-pyrotechnic devices include an orange distress flag and an electric distress light capable of flashing the S. O. S. distress signal (dot-dot-dot, dash-dash-dash, dot-dot-dot). The orange flag must be at least three feet by three feet, with a black square and ball on the orange background. (Distress signals change somewhat from inland to international use.)
- Boats with machinery, or engine driven, must have adequate ventilation; if gasoline driven, there must be a blower fitted to remove fumes from the bilge.
- A backfire flame arrester must be fitted to the intake mouth of the carburetor.
- The fuel system must be properly installed; the hose carrying fuel must be Coast Guard approved fuel hose.

- There are restrictions on fuel tanks, whether they are portable or permanently fitted. The Coast Guard recognizes a tank of seven gallons or less to be portable. Only Coast Guard approved tanks are legal. Permanent fuel tanks must be vented to the outside of the hull; permanent tanks and lines must be free of corrosion and not leak.

- The boat has to have at least one anchor, and anchor line adequate for the size of the vessel.

- Vessels less than sixteen feet in length must carry an alternate way to propel them in the event the engine dies. A paddle or oars will suffice, or you may use a complete spare engine with its own gasoline tank.

- All vessels must carry on board a manual dewatering device (portable bilge pump, bucket, scoop, etc.,) for manually bailing water, in addition to any electric or mechanical pump that may be fitted in the boat.

- The operator is responsible for the vessel being in top operating condition.

- All safety equipment should be on board.

- There should be no tripping hazards or sharp edges exposed.

- There should be no fire hazards, and the bilges should be clean.

- The galley is an important area, and must meet all safety standards. Appliances, stoves, etc., and their fuel supplies must be properly secured and not leak. No odor of fuel must be detected when the system is turned on. There must be no flammable material in the vicinity of the stove or heater. Only common appliance fuels may be used. Gasoline, benzene, or naphtha are not allowed because of their explosive nature. Appliance fuel shut-off safety valves must be installed and be readily accessible. Also, adequate ventilation is a must for the stove area and for the fuel supply.

- Each boat must be registered, and must display the assigned numbers on each side of the bow. Larger vessels may be documented and registered with the Coast Guard, but most small boats are numbered by the Department of Motor Vehicles. Some states are lenient regarding the size the vessel must be before registration is required. Check the regulations of the state in which you live.

- Electrical systems must be in good condition, with no wiring frayed or exposed. Fuses or circuit breakers must protect all circuits. Fuses or switches should be protected from rain or spray. Batteries must be properly secured and have adequate ventilation. Also, the batteries should be covered to prevent accidental arcing.

- All recreational boats that have a toilet must have an operable marine sanitation device or waste-holding tank installed. Under 65 feet in length, a boat may use a type one, two, or three sanitation treatment system, though over 65 feet, it must have a type two or three. All sanitation devices must be Coast Guard approved. The Coast Guard will check to see that you do not have a toilet that pumps straight overboard; if you do, they may close the valve and put a seal on the valve so that it cannot be used.

- Your boat must display a placard warning of the penalties for discarding trash or oil in U.S. waters. This placard must tell the limits of disposing of garbage and waste in U.S. waters, and of the prohibition of pumping oil out of any bilge into the water, a practice subject to heavy fines and possible jail sentences. This placard must be placed in a visible position.

- A copy of the navigation rules must be carried on any boat twelve meters (thirty-nine feet, four inches long) or larger.

- If you are licensed, carrying passengers for hire, the life preservers must be the special type with reflector tape sewn on, the type that keeps you floating with your face up. They must be stowed in a locker that is easy to get at; this locker must be marked on the outside, "Life Preservers."

- Emergency flares for day and night use must be properly stored; their expiration date must be legible.

- An E.P.I.R.B—"emergency position indicator radio beacon" transmitter—is necessary if you are going offshore.

- You must carry a VHF radio with channel 16, which you are supposed to monitor at all times.

- There must be an automatic fire extinguisher system in the engine room.
- You must carry a life raft or float suitable for the number of passengers aboard.
- Your boat must be equipped with a first-aid kit, and the captain must understand how to use the contents.

If some of the regulations mystify you, the U.S. Coast Guard will be very helpful and will explain exactly what you need. There is a Boating Safety Hotline, 1-800-368-5647.

I know that some people complain about Coast Guard boardings, but I have been boarded by them a few times in my life, and have always found them most courteous and helpful. As a general rule, they are mainly concerned with your safety, looking for anything on your yacht that may be a potential danger, or for safety equipment that you do not have on board but should.

The U.S. Coast Guard has made rules and regulations to cover most of the problems that might crop up in boating, but if you are venturing offshore, you should carry even more safety equipment, especially a means of retrieving a person who has fallen overboard. This can be a difficult problem, as I said earlier; even very experienced sailors have been unsuccessful at picking up a person in the water and lost them to drowning, even though they had the boat almost alongside the person a number of times.

One very good product on the market is the Lifesling, a horseshoe-type life ring bridled to a long line, the end of which is fastened to the boat and is easily deployed, then towed along like a ski tow line. The yacht is turned, making a circle around the person in the water until the line comes to them; when the Lifesling reaches them, the long bridle lines are easy to put over the head, bringing the life ring around the body. The crew of the yacht can then pull the person up close alongside. The Lifesling even makes it possible to hoist the person on board with the boom and winch, if they are not capable of climbing up themselves. This is often the case, especially if the person has been in cold water for a time.

The Coast Guard does not insist on your carrying a GPS, but this is a very necessary piece of safety equipment. It is hard to get in trouble if you know exactly where you are and what direction you are going.

Carrying passengers for hire offshore, you must have an EPIRB. But ordinary cruising yachts should always have one on board, and I'm sure most carry them. EPIRB transmitters have saved many lives, and in the unlikely event of your having to abandon ship, starting an EPIRB transmitting makes the chance of your having to spend many days, weeks, even months in a lifeboat, about zero. All airplanes, ships, and Coast Guard stations, among others, monitor the EPIRB distress frequency, and help is on the way in a matter of hours.

When the EPIRB is activated, it must be left on continuously. I read of a life-raft survivor who, to save the battery, had turned the transmitter off every now and then. This delayed his being picked up for days, because every time a ship or airplane was honing in on the distress signal, it stopped transmitting. This happened time and again until the transmitter's battery went dead, though by this time there was a full-blown search going on, and eventually the unfortunate sailor was found and picked up.

There are numerous EPIRB transmitters on the market. The simplest one must be switched on to activate the beeping signal, and this will indicate there is a person in distress, that is all. The most sophisticated model is capable of manual switch-on, but also switches itself on if it touches water. It automatically releases itself from the holding base if it is submerged. It will identify the particular vessel in distress, the owners, and just exactly where the vessel in distress is now.

With the best satellite EPIRB, help can be on the way in not much more than one hour. What a wonderful item to have along, since it is Murphy's law that if you are totally prepared for a particular emergency, it will never happen.

If you have a VHF radio installed, which is necessary, you must have a current FCC Marine Radio License. It is nice to have on board a powerful high-seas radio, with which to keep in contact with friends or relatives. This can also be used in case of emergency, to summon help.

Many sailors have a ham radio on board, and contact a radio net every day at certain times. This is a wonderful system to be involved in. Each sailor checks in at the outset of the voyage, telling information about his boat, destination, route, weather where he is, wind speed and wind direction, the speed he or she is making, and any other pertinent facts. Each day you can hear all this information about the weather each sailor is experiencing in the area he is sailing, so you have a good idea what to expect. There is almost always a cruiser up ahead traveling the same course you are.

For anyone even a little nervous about being a long way out of sight of land, it is a great comfort to have a ham radio and be on the net every day. Of course, there are great strides being made in the communications field today, with satellite systems making it possible to just pick up the phone and talk to anyone in the world or send faxes or E-mail to anyone with a fax machine or computer ready to receive them. All this makes it possible to stay in constant touch no matter where you go.

Another necessity for cruising is a safety harness for each crew member, a type of harness resembling a little kiddie's rein harness. The sailor's type has a length of line attached firmly to the harness; a snap hook is fastened to the end of the line, with which the sailor attaches himself or herself to the boat so securely that if the crew person falls overboard, they are still attached to the boat. If the crew person is wearing a safety harness latched to the boat, he is in no danger of being lost.

It is a good idea to run a heavy line the length of the yacht, fastened securely at each side to bow and stern; you can latch your safety harness to this line if you have to go up on deck or all the way forward in rough weather. This will keep you attached to the boat no matter what. Having the line attached only at the stern and the bow saves your having to change the latching hooks from lifeline to lifeline as you pass each stanchion. Even using a double-hook safety harness, it is sometimes difficult to do this switching past the stanchions, especially in inclement weather, in a squall with driving rain that hinders your visibility.

While we are on the subject of being prepared for the worst, a good life raft will give peace of mind. There are many to choose from. The simplest is a self-inflating rubber raft just big enough to hold onto, if there are more people than can get into the raft. There are large rafts with all kinds of stores: oars, a patching kit, a fishing kit, a first-aid kit, sea stores of water and food, an automatically inflated canopy with built-in radar reflector screens, a packed EPIRB, a small hand-operated water maker, and almost anything else you want. The only limitation is the weight of the life raft if you have to hand-launch it or lift it over a rail.

Life rafts should be checked and repacked by the manufacturer according to their recommendations. When it comes time to return the life raft for service and repacking, pull the ring and watch it inflate. I read of a person who each year sent his life raft back for repacking, and one time decided to see it inflated. However, when he jerked the ring, it wouldn't start the automatic cycle. On further inspection, he learned that the pull wire had a swageing on it, which could not come through the fiberglass canopy in which the raft was stored. In an emergency, this raft would have been totally useless. One wonders how this could have happened. Did the service people never pull the ring? Or did they just take it apart and repack it the same way as before?

Finally, before setting off on a cruise to foreign shores, especially in the tropics, it is important to obtain a copy of *Dangerous Marine Animals* or a similar book and study what organisms, plants, or animals to avoid. In the western Pacific a scuba diver was playing with a little blue octopus. He put it around his neck, was bitten by this very poisonous creature, and died shortly afterwards.

(For a discussion on another dangerous marine creature, the Crown of Thorns starfish, see page 123.)

CREW OVERBOARD RECOVERY 8

I talked before about the importance of crew-overboard recovery drill to teach each and every crew person to bring the boat back to a person in the water, within the least possible time. In the United States each year there are an average of eight hundred deaths in recreational boating, mostly caused by drowning, demonstrating that water can be very dangerous for an unprepared boater. Various are the reasons for these deaths: falling overboard, boats capsizing, collisions, boats sinking.

If a person enters the water, it is absolutely imperative that he or she be recovered without delay, before drowning or hypothermia occurs. Many of the accidental overboard victims may have been saved, if they had been retrieved immediately by competent crew.

Speed in recovery is imperative, especially if the water is cold. Hypothermia, the abnormal loss of body heat, occurs rapidly in water—twenty-five times faster than in air of equivalent temperature. Hypothermia causes loss of judgment and motor skills, eventually unconsciousness. Hypothermia can even become a problem in waters eighty degrees or more, though the warmer the water, the longer it takes for hypothermia to set in and cause problems—sometimes many hours, instead of minutes in cold water.

There are precautions boaters should take when the weather looks like it is deteriorating, or if a person is not comfortable in the water. Wear a flotation jacket or life preserver when you are boating. Wearing a flotation device greatly increases your chance of survival. There are lots of comfortable flotation jackets on the market nowadays. They even look sharp.

A problem can arise if a person falls overboard without the crew on board knowing. It is wise to always wear a safety harness with the line latched onto the boat. Certainly this is a must if you are single-handing a passage, because the boat will keep on sailing away from you if you are not connected to it. I cannot imagine a more depressing feeling than to be treading water hundreds or thousands of miles from land, and watching your yacht sailing on course, away from you.

A yacht I once sailed to New Zealand had a long line with a large loop tied in the bitter end, which dragged behind the boat while sailing. The inboard end was fastened to a cleat on the aft deck, but shortened with a heavy shock cord. If a crew person fell overboard, they had to immediately swim across the stern wake and grab the trailing line. The weight of the person hanging onto the line stretched the shock cord and pulled a clip off a switch, which immediately set off an alarm bell, alerting the crew. If the person could hold onto the line at the large knot until the crew got the boat stopped, it would be a simple matter of hauling in the person in the water.

Different sailing schools have taught maneuvering techniques to use after a person has fallen overboard. The figure eight, taught by A.S.A sailing schools, is to immediately sail on a broad reach away from the victim in the water, then after five to seven boat lengths, tack and drop back onto the same track as before or lower. Approach the victim from leeward, rounding the boat up into the wind to slow the forward movement as you get close to the person in the water.

Some people think that sailing six or seven boat lengths away from the victim is too far and takes up precious time. Modern Sailing Academy in Sausalito, California, teaches a faster return, similar to the figure eight taught by A S A, but sailing away only two or three boat lengths before tacking around to get back to the victim. If you have a "Lifesling" on board, the crew drops it over the stern and the boat makes circles around the victim until he or she gets the line in hand. One drawback to this maneuver is that if the sails are still up, the boat must jibe, maybe a number of times, and if jibes are not well controlled, damage can result to the sails or rigging.

Crew overboard recovery techniques must include a way for the crew, still on the boat, to get the person out of the water and up on deck. This can be difficult if the person has been in the water so long that they cannot help themselves. In this case, the crew must rig some type of hoisting sling, and all this takes time, especially if the crew have never practiced this essential part of recovery.

The beauty of the "Lifesling" is that once the person in the water has put the flotation collar over their head and gotten it under their arms, they are ready to be hoisted aboard. This can be done with the aid of a block on the boom and a winch, even if the person is helpless from injury or hypothermia.

Many captains practice getting the boat back to a "person" in the water, but it is just as important to include in the drill the means by which the person will be hauled on board. As the Boy Scouts say, "Be Prepared." Usually when you have everything ready for a disaster, it doesn't ever happen.

Spares to Carry 9

It is important that you make yourself as self-sufficient as possible if you are venturing offshore, more so if your plans include a long ocean crossing, when you may be on your own for weeks or months at a time.

A well-equipped cruising yacht should have three or more anchors and at least two anchor rodes, one being all chain. There may be times you will need two anchors set. If you lose one, having started off with only two, now you are down to only one anchor.

The problems may start if you are in an area with poor holding ground and are dependent on your one and only grip on the bottom, with a strong onshore wind, or even a hurricane brewing. Then you must weigh anchor and head out to sea.

If you cannot get the anchor up and have to abandon it until later, the all-chain rode should have a heavy nylon line joining the bitter end of the chain to the chain locker. The chain end will then come up on deck; you can tie a line as long as the depth of the water to the end of the chain, with a marker buoy or empty water bottle tied to the end of the line. Now you can cut the nylon line, which ties the chain to the chain locker, and drop everything overboard. Your anchor and chain are buoyed so that you can return when the weather is better and retrieve them.

Spare parts should be carried for the automatic pilot, even if you know nothing about electronics. So many parts now are simple plug-in modules, you can change each module one by one, and possibly you will be lucky.

The instruction books for each piece of equipment on board are a necessity. Often the book will explain exactly what to do to troubleshoot the problem. The mechanic's instruction manual should be obtained from the engine manufacturer to supplement the owner's handbook, which is very limited in specific information.

Spare parts for the engine should include gaskets for cylinder heads, valve covers, manifolds, exhausts, and water pumps, and extra gasket material from which you can make others that you may not have thought about.

The engine is extremely important. Besides propelling the boat, it also drives the alternator that charges the batteries. You must keep the batteries charged for lighting, autopilot operation, and so forth. Therefore, if the engine suffers a breakdown, you must have the necessary parts to fix it and get it going again.

Spare zincs should be on board, including the small pencil zincs that are in the heat exchangers, to prevent electrolysis. If these zincs are not in place and are not replaced regularly, the solder or brazing in the heat exchanger will dissolve into the salt water and the exchanger will leak, allowing salt water to enter the engine or transmission; either condition creates real problems. If the heat exchanger does not have zincs installed, it is necessary to have threaded flanges brazed or soldered into the exchanger, to allow screwing in the necessary pencil zincs.

On the list should also be spare impellers for any water pumps aboard, especially cooling water-circulating pumps, without which the engine will overheat.

You should carry at least one spare fan belt for every fan belt on the boat: the line shaft driving other accessories, the deck wash pump, air conditioning compressor, extra alternators or generators, and freezer or refrigerator compressor. If the engine installation has multiple belts, where you may have to remove two or three pieces of equipment to get to a defective belt, you can install the spare inner belts in place, tied back with plastic wire ties, the type that electricians use to bundle wiring. If you have a failure on the high seas, where it is so difficult to work, you do not need to take the outer equipment off. Simply unclip the spare belt, loosen the adjusting mechanism, and replace the old belt with the new one, and save yourself the labor of removing the equipment fitted in front of the inner belts.

You should carry enough engine oil to make the necessary oil changes to fit your boat's fuel requirements, also oil filters and fuel filters for the same number of changes. With diesel engines especially, it is good practice to change the fuel filter every time the engine oil is changed.

If you have no hand suction pump at the galley to bring fresh water from the water tanks but have instead a twelve-volt electric pressure water pump, you should carry an extra pressure switch and an extra drive belt, if it is a belt-drive type pump, or carry a complete spare fresh-water pump similar to the one installed. When the spare pump is identical to the pump in use, you do not have to make any modifications to the plumbing.

It is also handy to have a salt-water pump at the galley sink. This will help save fresh water, since you can do 90 percent of the dish and pot washing in salt water, then just a quick rinse in fresh water. Spares for this pump are not so critical; you can always get a bucket of salt water from over the side.

Bilge pumps should have a spare control switch and float switch; maybe a complete spare pump is a good idea. If you are going to spend the money for a complete pump, you should spend a little more for plumbing, and install the spare pump with its own float switch somewhere above the bilge pump you already have in place. Then in an emergency, or if the bilge pump fails, the second pump will automatically start up and keep you afloat, without your having to go hunt out the spare, install it, and wire it up before it can start pumping.

Actually, I have seen a beautiful 44-foot sailing yacht saved from sinking by this kind of setup, when the lower small bilge pump's float switch failed and excessive water was leaking into the boat through the propeller shaft stuffing box. Because the large second pump was installed in a larger space than in the bottom of a small bilge, quite a few gallons of water had filled the bilge, almost up to the cabin sole, but the second pump kept the water from getting any higher. No important equipment like the engine or transmission was damaged.

Since there is always the possibility of hitting something underwater, thereby damaging the propeller, it is a good idea to carry a spare prop and also a propeller puller, since it is very difficult to get the broken propeller off the taper of the shaft, unless a puller is available. Some cruisers even carry a spare propeller shaft in case the obstruction bends the shaft as well as damaging the propeller. These can be really expensive to replace, especially if you are a long way away from civilization and have to send for new ones from halfway around the world.

I once met a crew member of a 55-foot yacht that had lost its mast in the Tuamotus, in French Polynesia, and he told me it was costing $85,000.00 to have a new mast sent out from the U.S.A.—and that was in 1973. Of course, you cannot carry a spare mast, but you can see how important it is to carry spares.

Navigation lights are necessary as well as required by law, so it is important to carry spare bulbs; also spare bulbs for other lamps are a good idea, and spare batteries for flashlights. Rechargeable batteries are even better. Carry spare fuses to replace any fuses installed in your boat.

A voltage tester, even a fairly simple one, should be in the tool kit, which should have a wide variety of tools.

If you have no way to generate 120 volt a/c electricity, you can get a small propane soldering gun. You never know what you might have to work on, and it is not so difficult if you have the tools to do the job.

If you have only one source of battery charging on your engine, you should carry a spare alternator and voltage regulator, if it is not built into the alternator. It may be a good idea to carry a spare starter motor, if funds allow this expense. A starter motor usually does not give out suddenly, but instead shows signs of weakening by cranking the engine slower and slower over a long period of time.

Carry spare spark plugs for the dinghy's outboard motor and fuel filters for this motor, as well as a supply of outboard motor oil. Take a supply of waste rags, paper towels, or wipers, in addition to plastic bags to help with clean-up in the engine room. There is always a little oil or fuel spilled when you change filters and such.

Some places you may want to take on fresh water but cannot get close to the faucet. It is great to have a couple of long garden hoses on board.

You also may be in an area where it is impossible to reach a faucet when you are anchored out, so it is necessary to have some water jars that you can take to shore in the dinghy and fill. Ideal for this purpose are those thin plastic four- or five-gallon water jugs, which, when empty, can be collapsed and packed away in a fairly small space. On our trips I took twenty one-gallon antifreeze plastic containers filled almost to the top with fresh water. These were all tied together through the handles, then tied with a slipknot across the aft deck near the life raft. In the highly unlikely event of having to abandon ship, these twenty-gallon bottles could be thrown into the life raft, or even into the sea, to be retrieved from the life raft later; they will float, fresh water being lighter than salt water.

When we were anchored in the lagoons of the South Pacific, the gallon water jars came in very handy as a fresh-water shower immediately after swimming, with one gallon being used by each person. They were also an easy way for the junior crewmembers to take the empty jugs ashore for refilling, a chore they seemed to enjoy.

A dry-charged battery is another item that may be a nice thing to have along, if there is space and money available.

We were anchored in Nuku Hiva, when into the anchorage sailed a 46-foot ketch, silently dropping the anchor. The owners, a delightful couple from Connecticut, were sailing around the world in their late sixties.

Later we were to find out that the yacht had suffered a saltwater leak from the exhaust system, a leak that poured over the alternator, destroying its charging capabilities. Their batteries were dead, and the engine could no longer be started.

Jozo and I repaired the exhaust cooling water leak, then removed the alternator and disassembled it, only to find all the wiring's terminals had been corroded off by electrolysis. We cleaned everything up and reterminated each wire. As we reattached each to the farthest terminal (neither of us was an electrician), I asked Jozo what were the chances of this alternator working, and he replied "I'd say less than no chance." I was feeling the same.

However, when we had everything together, we wondered how we were going to get a battery to start the engine. We did not have jumper cables long enough to reach from *Seahorse* to their engine room, even if we came alongside. Each of the batteries in *Seahorse* weighed 150 pounds, a lot to hassle out of the boat and into a dinghy. However, the owner George said, "I have a dry-charged 12-volt battery we can use," and produced a brand new battery from a locker. He added a bottle of electrolyte, and in a little while the battery was charged and ready.

We started the diesel, which roared into life immediately, and lo and behold, the charge needle was reading 40 amps. Both Jozo and I were amazed, and the owner was delighted. He stared at the refrigeration light that indicated that the freezer was operating and soon he would have ice for his drinks.

We were rewarded with a most delightful dinner at the best restaurant in Papeete, when we all met later in Tahiti.

This was my first experience with dry-charged batteries, and I thought it was a great idea. If all batteries were dead, it would be wonderful to have an ace in the hole like a dry-charged battery that stays dormant until the electrolyte is added.

Food is the last provision to be stored aboard, and the lists can be long and complicated. You must consider where to put the boxes and boxes that will litter the deck, and the dock, for the last few days before you set sail.

There are food lists to prepare. It would help to read Eric Hiscock's *Cruising Under Sail*. Many feel that this work, comprising over 500 pages, is the most comprehensive book ever written on the subject. Eric wrote in great detail, giving food lists for two or more. It takes quite a lot of planning to cover everything you have to carry along, and a lot depends on the tastes of the permanent members of the cruise.

We had *Seahorse* all loaded and ready to leave in 1973 when Jozo, the last to arrive on departure day, showed up with 48 six-packs of beer and two full cases of brandy. For a time, every locker door you opened, revealed cans or bottles. Eventually, with the help of others, Jozo was able to get rid of them all. We ate and drank our way across the Pacific Ocean.

COOKING AT SEA 10

I am probably the last one in the world who should write about cooking. I can cook to survive, and make a fair stab at turning out a meal, but making a fancy gourmet meal is completely beyond me. Fancy sauces are not in my vocabulary, though I enjoy them. However, there are a few things I have learned about preparing meals on the high seas. Even when the seas get unbearably rough, you still get hungry.

I have found that it is well worthwhile to prepare certain foods while still in port, before the trip begins. For the first few days, it is wonderful to have a large pot of good rich soup or stew--not too highly seasoned, though, as stomachs are very tender until you get your sea legs. This can be easily heated as a one-pot meal, which simplifies the cooking chore while you don't feel so good.

If your boat has a good freezer, many meals can be prepared ahead of the departure day, packaged according to the number of crew that will be eating. As long as these packages are well marked, it is a simple task to pick out what you want to eat, pop it in the microwave oven, and presto, you have a meal, with almost no work.

Without a microwave, you have to think ahead as to what you want to eat. Remove it from the freezer, allowing enough time to thaw out, then cook in the normal way.

Salads, or the fixings of a salad, may be prepared at the dock also, using Ziploc bags filled with washed and cleaned salad lettuce, chopped or diced green peppers, onions, cabbage, and many other delights that you might prefer. As long as you have a refrigerator, these things last pretty well. Lettuce can be stored in plastic bags or boxes as long as these are not allowed to freeze.

I have found the best way to use lettuce is to take, say, ten large heads and use only the outside leaf off each lettuce each day, since these are the first to start to decay. This way you gradually eat the outsides of all the lettuce and eventually have only the little hearts of ten lettuce left to eat. How many heads of lettuce you bring along depends, of course, on how many people are aboard. If you judge things right you can have nice salads for quite a few days.

There should be a number of different ways to cook on board, if the trip is going to be an extended one. If the only stove you have breaks down, it can make things quite miserable if a hot meal cannot be prepared. The regular stove should be accompanied by at least a Primus stove, which may only be a small one-pot heater but can still save the day, even if it takes longer to make a dinner.

We found a pressure cooker pot extremely useful, and a pressure cooker saves quite a lot of fuel; this in itself makes it a big help, since you are always trying to stretch your supplies, especially when away from land and no stores are available. One thing to watch when using the pressure cooker is the danger of the little pressure-release hole being blocked by a particle of food. This can be very dangerous if the lid is unscrewed to lift off the pot, and steam under pressure gushes out all over the cook. I know this for a fact, since I had a crewman cooking dinner in a swimsuit. We were in the tropics, and though we had a large plastic apron in the galley, he was not using it. He opened the lid and was badly burned over his bare chest.

We doctored his burns carefully, but a week later when we reached the Islands, he was still suffering with two or three spots that were infected. We took him to the little grass shack hospital. They fixed him right up, dressed his wounds, gave him antibiotics, served him dinner, kept him overnight, and the next day when we picked him up the bill was $10.00 U.S.

So make sure the pressure is all released before opening the pressure cooker.

A charcoal barbeque is a very popular way to cook, and can also be a good back-up way to prepare a meal. Also one fuelled by propane can be carried if you have propane aboard.

Those lucky enough to have electricity generated by the main engine or a separate generator set will be able to cook by electricity, which can be helpful in keeping the boat cooler in the tropics. A microwave oven can cook lots of dishes without creating much excess heat in the cabin. An electric skillet connected by an extension cord and left up on deck or in the cockpit can prepare quite a variety of foods without heating the cabin at all.

Each type of stove has its advocates; each has its own benefits and drawbacks. Alcohol stoves are felt by many oldtimers to be the safest type of stove, since a fire can easily be doused with water. However, alcohol does not put out a lot of BTU's for the fuel consumed, and sometimes it takes quite a while to boil a large pot of water. One other drawback is the fact that spilled alcohol can burn without your seeing the flame, and you can be badly burned by the time the pain starts.

Kerosene stoves are another good choice, giving a lot of heat and being easily adjusted, almost like gas. The stove burner must be preheated by filling the little cup below the burner with alcohol. Light the alcohol, and when the alcohol is almost burned away, the kerosene valve should be hot enough to change the kerosene spray into a gas as the burner control knob is opened very slowly. If all is done right, the burner will light with a hot blue flame. This is fairly simple to do once you get used to it, but many people feel it's a bit of a chore, since it occasionally takes a couple of tries to get the stove burning correctly.

Diesel stoves, almost always a favorite among commercial fishermen, can range from a simple drip burner heating a cooking surface of flat cast iron, to a fairly sophisticated, thermostatically controlled type that has an automatic burner with light sensors that shut off the fuel if the flame goes out for any reason. They can heat the water, and pump the hot water through the yacht to heat radiators, thus warming the boat. A diesel stove is possibly the safest stove you could have, excepting electricity. The big drawback to a diesel stove is the heat it creates in the cabin. This can be wonderful if you are cruising Alaska or Antarctica, but a real problem when you are cruising the tropics.

Propane is a very easy way to cook, especially if the stove has an automatic sparker to light the gas. Just turn on the burner and poof, it is lit and ready to cook, and as easily adjusted as any gas range in your home. The propane system must be very carefully installed, with the tanks fitted outside the hull in a deck box or equivalent. It should have a shut-off valve where it comes into the hull to stop any possibility of gas getting inside the boat unless you are cooking. This valve should always be turned off immediately cooking is halted.

Propane, being heavier than air, will settle in the bilge if any gas is leaked from the system. This gas in the bilge is literally a bomb ready to explode if an automatic pump goes on or anything causes a spark to ignite the gas. It is almost a necessity to have a gas sniffer system installed, with the sensor fitted in the lower part of the boat. This will sound a warning if gas is present, which will make life much safer.

There is the story of the parachute jumper who, after both of his parachutes failed to open, falls to earth. As he falls, he sees a speck hurtling up from earth. As the speck gets closer he recognizes it's a man, and he yells, "Do you know anything about parachutes?" To which the man coming upward replies, "No, do you know anything about propane stoves?"

Many people have been seriously hurt, if not killed by propane in a boat, so it is not a funny subject. Great care must be taken with this system.

Probably the safest means of cooking is using electricity to power a microwave, hot plates, an electric skillet, and the like. But not everyone has a generating system on board. Though it is possible to install an inverter giving 120 volts from a twelve-volt system, this system needs the engine running and a large-capacity alternator pumping amps into the battery system. Still, it is nice to have an inverter and be able to get 120 volts occasionally, even if it will not power everything you would like.

Ocean sailing creates difficulties for the cook, since the boat is seldom steady. Pots can slide and fall, and their contents can spill, making a slippery mess on the cabin sole. This will be very dangerous, and who is going to clean up that mess? It helps a lot if the stove is fitted on gimbals so it can swing and level itself no matter at what angle the boat is heeled.

I have used both types, gimbaled and non-gimbaled, and much prefer the gimbaled type. Of course, if the weather is at all inclement, pots should not be filled more than halfway, to allow for any movement or sudden jerking of the stove.

Whether you have a swinging or stationary stove, it must have fiddlerails, which can be set to hold a pot or pan firmly over the burner, not allowing it to slide in any way.

A waist-high safety strap or rope should be attached firmly to the counter at one side of the stove, with a hook or snap shackle on the end, also a ring base on the other side of the stove. This enables the cook to put the rope or strap around his or her back and latch the hook or snap to the ring. This holds the cook securely by the stove while allowing him to turn sideways towards a sink or counter, but preventing his being off balance with a pot of boiling water or food.

Good ventilation above or near the stove makes life much more tolerable for the cook, especially in the tropics.

Eating is a necessary part of life; we cannot exist for long without food. It is therefore good to give a lot of thought to preparing your galley to make it as easy as possible for you to prepare food even in difficult conditions.

SAILING

PART TWO

CRUISING

Sailing

TAHITI, EVERY SAILOR'S DREAM 11

"Don't go near Papeete," we were advised in 1973 when heading for the South Pacific, "because of the noise and pollution that civilization has brought to Tahiti." But just the name Tahiti conjures up all kinds of dreams for most of us. Certainly most males dream of friendly native girls in grass skirts, dancing the Tamarae, with swaying hips and expressive hand gestures. This tropical paradise has been described time and time again. So after dreaming about sailing there for years, I was determined to see for myself.

Our course from San Francisco brought us to Nuku Hiva in the Marquesas Islands, three thousand two hundred miles from San Francisco. The first time we sailed between the East and West Sentinel Rocks, which mark the entrance to Taiohai bay on the southern coast of the island of Nuku Hiva, the northern entering port of the Marquesas Islands, a large, easily navigated inlet lay before us, calm and beautifully serene, especially to a crew twenty-three days out of sight of land. Only one yacht was anchored in the bay, near the small village of Taiohai. It belonged to a charming Frenchman named Max, who was single-handing around the world. It was a delight when he came over and greeted us with an armful of Pamplamoose, the local grapefruit, the largest and sweetest we had ever tasted. The date was March 1973.

The Island of Nuku Hiva, like all the Marquesan Islands, was rugged and mountainous, with great peaks rising from the sea and stretching up into the clouds. The ground cover was lush with vegetation so dense it looked like green velvet. Because of the terrain, there was not a road around the island to connect the few villages. They were only accessible by boat.

Taiohai was a friendly little town, with around five hundred inhabitants, and every evening the whole populace gathered at the pavilion on the beach to sing and dance the Tamarae, with much hip swinging and laughter. They also danced the original Marquesan dance, with the men uttering deep guttural chants as they danced.

We were told that these dances were done not so long ago in history, when the Marquesans were cannibals who ate their enemies, supposedly to gain the enemies' strength. (Cannibalism has been outlawed for a long time, but the last case recorded was in the middle nineteen thirties.)

The Polynesians practice dancing all year long, hoping to be ready to participate in the contests held in July during the Bastille Day Celebrations. The drums they dance to are hollowed-out logs, which they beat so fast, with only one stick, it is almost impossible to see their hands move.

When a cruise ship came into the bay, the villagers put on a real show, dancing and giving the tourists flower leis, also spreading out their wares for sale, which included pareaus (large flowered wrap-around cloth material worn by many Polynesian women), shells, and wonderful wood carvings.

The only business visible was the local store owned by Maurice McKitterick. Yachtsmen have been writing about Maurice for years. He stocked everything: hardware, canned goods, groceries, vegetables, fishing tackle, diesel fuel, gasoline, and best of all, cold drinks and beer. At only eight degrees south of the equator, the climate is fairly hot, so the cold drinks were most welcome at all times of the day. There was also a bakery, run by a Chinese man, so fresh French bread was available every day.

Maurice did not appear to bother keeping fruit, probably because various types grew all over the place. We walked a little way inland and were able to pick fresh pamplamoose, papaya, mango, breadfruit, and bananas. Of course coconuts were lying around everywhere.

When we visited Nuku Hiva again in 1984 we expected things to be a little different, and sure enough, as we sailed up into the bay, there were over twenty sailboats from all over the world, and numerous local fishing boats, all anchored in the same bay off Taiohai village.

Ashore, business was booming. Maurice was still in business, but had now the competition of five other stores.

There were now two hotels, two restaurants, a local television cable channel, and lots of motor scooters and other vehicles running back and forth displaying prosperity. Even the little church had been replaced with a beautiful stonework church that looked more like a cathedral.

The population had grown to about twelve hundred, and although shy, they were still a delightful, friendly people. We were sad to find that the thrilling Polynesian dancing had almost been replaced by modern disco.

At one time the old charts showed the place to anchor was in front of the Governor's mansion, but now yachts were required to anchor to the west of a large white stone marker on shore.

Taiohai bay is a large, well-protected anchorage, but since there is no barrier reef around the island, there is at times quite a surge, causing almost surf at the beach. At times this makes dinghy landing quite exciting.

One particular day as we approached the beach in our dinghy, the waves were surging up the beach. I said, "Now, the second the bow touches the beach, everyone jump out, grab a lifting handle, pick up the 12-foot rubber boat, and run up the beach until we are clear of the surf." This we did and it worked like a charm. So we tied the bowline to a palm tree and walked to town for the well-deserved cold drink.

A few hours later on our return to the dinghy, I said, "Now we do the same thing again in reverse, O.K?" So we each grabbed a lifting handle, picked up the boat, and raced down the beach heading for the water, when suddenly the forgotten bowline became taut, the boat stopped dead in midair, and four burly sailors ran into the water sans dinghy. We looked around sheepishly, hoping no one had seen the experienced yachtsmen displaying such a feat of nonseamanship.

We continued on through the Tuamotus, or Dangerous Archipelago as they are called, to Rangiroa, the largest atoll in the group. Rangiroa is a delight to visit. Its two passes--the easterly one named Tipatu, and the westerly one, Avatoru--lead into the large lagoon. The passes are wide and deep, easily navigated except when the tide is running out. This makes a current of up to eight knots against you when you are coming into the lagoon.

Once we watched an 80-foot ketch (that we found out later was underpowered with only a 120 h.p. diesel) powering in the pass for over one hour before she made it in against the current. Small boats can usually sneak in, keeping close to the side of the pass and thus avoiding the strongest flow, which is clearly visible in the middle of the pass, running like a river.

We did not think Rangiroa would hold our interest for very long, since there are only two small towns, one at each end of the coral strip of land, which is only about five miles long. There is nothing taller than a palm tree on the whole island.

The lagoon is one of the largest in the world, stretching almost thirty miles, east to west, and close to fifteen miles north and south. It is relatively free of dangers to yachts, if care is taken. The water is crystal clear, and the many coral heads are mostly well under the surface. Those close enough to the surface to endanger a small yacht are very visible in the crystal-clear water. It helps if a person can go up the mast a little way, scanning the waters ahead, to warn the skipper of any dark patch in the water ahead.

One wonderful experience in Rangiroa is "drifting the pass." This is motoring in the dinghy out to the ocean end of the pass, with the tide coming in, then jumping over the side with mask, snorkel, and flippers, and just drifting all through the pass towards the lagoon. The dinghy drifts alongside.

Gliding over the crystal-clear water you see all kinds of marine life, from large sharks down near the bottom sixty feet below, at the outer end of the pass, to every kind of fish you could imagine, including many smaller varieties which come swimming nearby. As you drift farther in, it is almost as though you are in a giant aquarium with what looks like goldfish, three feet long, swimming alongside maybe only ten feet away.

The bottom of the pass, though over thirty feet down, is totally visible, with every shape, size, and color of the most beautiful coral. The scene fills you with awe and wonder. The sight of an occasional reef shark swimming below you, lends much excitement to this fantastic experience.

We anchored *Seahorse* off the Kia Ora Hotel, and found the management very friendly. We asked and were granted their permission to freely use their large dock for our dinghy landing, making it easy for us to go ashore. The Kia Ora was an easy place to spend time, and is a wonderful place for drinks, or coffee, after dinner.

Most of the land of this island lies between the two passes. This land is about five miles long by less than one mile wide. A small airport is situated in the middle, with service to and from Tahiti in smaller planes. There is a limit on the amount of baggage you can take on interisland flights.

The diving and snorkeling in Rangiroa is absolutely wonderful. The lagoon is well known for the abundance of marine life, including reef sharks, white tip, and black tip, that the natives say are nothing to worry about.

The Polynesian man who took hotel guests out for boat rides, was called Matahi. He was in charge of the hotel's boats and would give the guests a great show when using the glass-bottom boat. He would anchor over a coral garden, about thirty feet below the surface. Then he would go down and spear a large moray eel or other large fish, which he would bring up on board, dispatch, and hang over the side, tied by a strong rope and weighted to hold it down about twenty feet. Within seconds sharks came sniffing around, and eventually started biting at the dead fish. Matahi would come back up pretty quickly when the sharks started to get into a feeding frenzy.

These reef sharks seldom reach a length of more than eight feet, but they made me nervous. Though Matahi claimed they were not dangerous, I felt that if you ran across one that had a headache or was mad at the world, it could take out a big chunk of meat, if it attacked.

On a scuba dive with a friend, Greg, we were moving around the bottom sixty feet down when a white-tip shark came around, and when he swam directly towards us, I stretched out my arms and legs and yelled into my mouthpiece to scare him off. Well, he swam away but came right back, and we watched nervously as he came in closer and faster each time. Each time I did my yelling and stretching, to make myself as large as possible. This scenario continued as we slowly made our way up to the surface, the shark following us all the way. We got out of the water intact, though very nervous.

That evening we went ashore for coffee after dinner, and met Matahi. We related the story of our long shark encounter, saying, "You said they were not dangerous." He shrugged his massive shoulders and said that they weren't, unless they got into a feeding frenzy. I then asked him why it had come at us again and again. With a smile he replied, "Probably to see why you made noises and blew bubbles and spread out your arms."

Another day Greg decided to fish and caught a small one, which he used for bait. With it weighted down near the bottom, he hooked a four-foot shark. We got the shark up alongside, and not wanting to land him on the deck alive, we put a slip knot around his tail and hauled him up, using the main boom, leaving him hanging with his nose about two feet above the water.

We decided to leave the shark hanging while we ate dinner, and as usual, we went ashore to the hotel for coffee. We met Matahi and told him that we had caught the shark and planned on cutting off some fillets, cooking them to find out what shark tasted like.

However, Matahi became agitated, and flatly stated, "No, we do not eat shark. No, you don't eat this, no . . . no . . . !" So we said we would not.

I had always heard, and believed, that sharks must keep swimming to obtain oxygen from the water, so I was certain that our shark was dead after approximately three hours hanging high and dry. So we pulled the slip knot and it fell with a splash into the water. The shark seemed to roll over as though dead, but one second later with a flash of its tail, it was gone.

This was a lesson learned. A shark can be lying on your deck, you are sure it is dead, but as you walk past, it can really do serious damage to your leg or foot. Sharks obviously can survive for a long time out of the water.

The Tuamotus do not have any fresh water in the ground, probably because they are just above sea level; however, the people catch rainwater in large buildings which have roofs that don't reach out to the walls, so the rain water falls inside the building. These are called cisterns. Some of the natives also have wells. This seemed strange to me, since the land is only a few feet above sea level, but they told me that the rainwater settles on top of the salt water that always seeps in when they dig a well. I would have thought that the two waters would immediately mix, but they are careful to take the water from the top and they get good fresh water.

Rangiroa was a delightful place to spend time. It is really a diver's paradise, and a snorkeler's dream come true. We will always have wonderful memories of this island, and had no trouble staying there for a whole month.

We next headed for Papeete, the trade winds moving *Seahorse* quietly along at six knots. I still almost see that tropical night; it was unforgettable, with the warm gentle breezes scented by the flowers of nearby islands. We had left Rangiroa around six P.M. The sea was calm, the breeze gentle, and every star in the heavens shone so brightly that it was difficult to pick out the familiar constellations. It was one of those nights that makes it very difficult to go to bed, even if you have been up all day. When everything was going so well, it made all the work done to make the voyage possible, well worthwhile.

Next day we motored into Papeete harbor, a large enough bay to allow super-large ships to come in and tie alongside the international shipping quay, actually on an island called Motu Uta. A road and causeway connects this island area through the commercial area called Fare Ute, where most of the marine supply stores are located, within easy walking distance of the town of Papeete.

The quay where visiting yachts tie up stern-to, Mediterranean style, is right in the heart of town, and it is the most wonderful place in the world for people-watching.

Small French cars, Japanese cars, an occasional Mercedes or BMW, countless motor scooters whiz past on Boulevard Pomare. This is the main thoroughfare skirting Papeete harbor, and the traffic is an endless stream of noise and color--especially at commute times, which seem to stretch from seven A.M. 'till seven P.M. Look out when you cross the road. Though there are apparent crosswalks, the traffic does not seem to see them.

Papeete is a bustling city, with lots to see. It is a favorite stop-off for all kinds of cruise ships. Cargo ships come and go at all hours, bringing all the necessities to Tahiti and taking away copra, the dried white meat of the coconut, and other products. Copra is brought from the outer islands by interisland schooner (still so called, although they have not had sails for many years, but are actually small ships). It is possible to take a cruise around all the out islands and back, at a very reasonable cost. The interisland schooner cruise lasts about a month.

French navy ships come and go, and an occasional U.S. Navy ship will visit. The U.S.S. *Halsey* stopped for a time during our last stay in Papeete. We were varnishing rails and so forth, when a man called us from the dock. He saw our California hailing port on our transom, and said he was also from California--San Diego, actually. He looked like a sailor, so I asked him which boat he was on. He pointed along the quay and said the gray boat. I couldn't think which yacht was gray, and said so. He replied that his boat was called the *Halsey*. Definitely a big gray boat. He then asked us to be his guests for a tour of the *Halsey*, which we did the next day and enjoyed it very much.

One of the great attractions in Papeete is the market, housed in a giant warehouse, a two-story complex right in the heart of town. Every type of fruit, vegetable, bread, cakes, meat, and fish is available, and the market starts about five o' clock in the morning. The produce is wonderfully fresh, and when you buy a pineapple, it was just picked; it is ripe, and ready to eat immediately. Since they usually have pineapples, fruits, or vegetables tied up in bunches, it is common for yachties to share a bunch. They are so ripe, they don't keep too long, unless one has a lot of refrigerator space, which is not usual in a boat.

The market is completely Polynesian and is so colorful; it is a must on the list of things to see. The upper balcony has all kinds of Polynesian crafts, wood carvings, grass skirts and tops, shells, and many items you will not be able to go home without.

Close to the market is the local bus service depot; the vehicles are called "Le Truck," probably because they are made from a truck frame. This service may be the best transportation system I have ever seen. Most vehicles are owner-operated, so are well kept and clean, some with heavy-duty stereo systems and giant speakers. They run almost continuously, from around 4 o clock in the morning 'till midnight. Seldom do you have to wait more than a few minutes for a ride, and I have seen them detour off the route a mile or more, to leave an elderly Tahitian lady off right at her door, then run back to the regular route and continue on. They also will stop just about anywhere along the road to pick you up. Usually the second you walk out to the road they use, you will hear their horn tooting, to let you know they are there and available.

Le Truck services the road almost all around the island; the system is divided in two, with vehicles going in each direction, west and east, out from the depot. They meet at the other side of the island, near Tahiti Iti, the smaller part of Tahiti that makes up the figure eight, the shape of the island. There they turn around and head back to the depot, each in its own route.

There is really only one main road around the island; this road is about twenty-eight miles long with little roads branching inland where the mountains allow access. Lake Vaihiria nestles in a mountain crater at around three thousand feet elevation, in the southern end of Tahiti. Until recently it was accessible only after a long, arduous climb on foot, but there is now a seven-and-a-half-mile dirt road which makes the trip possible in four-wheel drive Jeep-type vehicles. It is said that the road will be left in this poor condition, to discourage a flood of picnic crowds polluting the area. It is hoped that this will preserve the natural beauty of the area, which is outstanding.

On the other side of Tahiti from Papeete is the interesting Paul Gauguin Museum, well worth the trip. Gauguin, born in Paris in 1848, eventually gave up everything and moved to Tahiti. He remained in French Polynesia for the rest of his life, painting the colorful Polynesian women and scenery. He died in one of the Marquesas Islands in 1903. The Museum houses most of his personal belongings. Many articles displayed describe his life in France and Polynesia.

Along the Boulevard Pomare, named after the Tahitian royal family, is the Protestant Church, and though the sermon is in Tahitian—and French, at times—the service is extremely enjoyable. The choir is divided, with the men sitting on one side of the church and the women on the other. The singing begins with the women singing the first verse, often only one woman singing the first line; then the men sing the next; then all join in together in the most beautiful harmony for the rest of the hymn.

The Tahitians dress for Sunday, the men in snow-white shirts and usually black dress slacks, these usually hiding the ever-present thongs. The women are in bright, colorful dresses, and wear the most beautiful hats, trimmed with flowers, or shells, or feathers.

Near the church, on the beach, is the area used by the racing canoes. These sport long, sleek hulls, many of them hollowed out of a single log, with outriggers for stability. The Polynesian crews, both men and women, practice all year long, skimming over the lagoon, sometimes softly chanting in deep guttural tones; then every fifth or sixth stroke, the lead paddler calls out a command and all the paddles are switched over to the other side, just like clockwork.

Bastille Day celebrations are held each year in July, marking the day the French people overthrew the French royal family. The celebrations last two weeks or more. The competitions, mostly held on the main islands, are organized for all kinds of sports; they bring competitors from even the farthest-out islands of French Polynesia. The most prominent events appear to be the canoe races, with both sexes competing separately in two-person, four-person, or six-person crews. At the final contests, competition is extremely fierce, with yelling, cheering, and canoes bumping into each other. You will even see canoes awash, with crews swimming alongside bailing them out.

They have spear throwing, hurling the long shafts up at a coconut fastened to the top of a thirty-foot-high pole. At first, you don't expect anyone to hit the coconut, but when all the participants have thrown, there are usually several spears stuck firmly in the coconut.

There are contests to see who is the fastest to split open a coconut and get out the white meat. Coconuts are very difficult to open; if you have ever tried it, you know just how tough they are. First the great outer husk has to be removed, then the shell broken, then the white coconut meat extracted. However, the contest to pick the winner for coconut meat extraction, will leave you wondering if you can believe your eyes. The Polynesians are masters at this; from start to finish it takes them only a few seconds.

The final contests are held in Papeete, though viewing the initial games in Bora Bora was absolutely wonderful, the center of festivities being around the quay, off the main town. The quay is prepared in the preceding weeks by the building of many little baranques, or grass shacks, which are used as restaurants and gift shops during the two weeks of the Bastille Day celebrations. They are then pulled down when all the celebrations are over.

There are some restrictions that yachtsmen have to observe in Papeete. There is a limit to the time you can stay tied to the quay; after the allotted time, the rate you pay to the port captain doubles. This is to discourage those who once stayed a year or more. However, you only have to go away for a day to Moorea, about three hours away, then back to Papeete, and if there is space at the quay, you start at the beginning rate again for another stay.

Moorea, within sight, resembles Bali Hai. A high-speed ferryboat will take you over to visit. Each way takes less than one hour. Many feel that Bora Bora and Moorea share the honors of being the most beautiful islands in the world. Having spent much time on both islands, I cannot decide which is better. The snorkeling is better in Bora Bora lagoon.

Papeete has changed a lot over the past fifty years. When Eric and Susan Hiscock first tied up to the quay they were surrounded by interisland schooners––with sails, no less. I am sure many would feel that it has changed for the worse, and each time I have visited, there is a little more noise, a little more pollution, more cars, and more motor scooters, but the magic is still there. It will be hard to spoil Paradise.

The Polynesians are still very friendly and helpful, though not forward. They will often ignore you in passing, but if you smile and greet them with the usual "bon jour" (good day), they are quick to respond with the same, or "iorana," the greeting in Tahitian.

Polynesians have held on to their culture, though they have adopted quite a lot from the French, using what they like and discarding the rest. We had a Roman Catholic nun, or Sister of Mercy, on board for dinner, and found her very interesting. She taught in the local school, and we quizzed her about the Church's feelings regarding the free and easy lifestyle of the Polynesians: having children by many partners, young girls having babies that are then raised by their mothers or grandmothers, and the general easy-going promiscuous lifestyle. She just shrugged her shoulders and stated that the Catholic Church did everything in its power to teach them proper behavior, but when nothing worked, they just had to go along and try to ignore it.

The Polynesians love to go to church on Sunday. They get all dressed up, catch up on all the gossip, and sing their heads off, but beyond that, they don't take anything too seriously. They are a very happy race of people. We will always have fond memories of Tahiti and her islands.

The Author

Seahorse II Sea Trials San Francisco Bay

Taio Hai Bay, Nuku Hiva, Marquesas Islands

Nuku Hiva

Nuku Hiva, Marquesas Islands

Rangiroa

Dolphin Playing, Rangiroa

Rangiroa, Tuomotu Islands

View from the Kia Ora Hotel, Rangiroa

Rangiroa

Rangiroa, Tuomotu Islands

Windbreaker out of Long Beach, California: Rangiroa

Rangiroa Lagoon

Papeete Harbor, Tahiti

Papeete Harbor, Tahiti

"Le Truck" Local Bus Service, Tahiti

Papeete Market

Steven Robinson Enjoying Paradise

Varnishing in Paradise

Seahorse II at Anchor, Moorea Lagoon

Moorea Lagoon

On the Beach, Bora Bora

Windrift, out of San Diego: Bora Bora Lagoon

Stopover at Plantation Island Resort, Nadi, Fiji

Plantation Island Resort, Nadi, Fiji

The Regent of Fiji Hotel

Mary With Her Personal Bodyguard

The Market in Suva, Fiji

One of the Many Temples in Suva

One of the Many Gorgeous Beaches in Fiji

After a Tough Day in Fiji

Sunset, Bora Bora

Bora Bora 12

Lying approximately 140 miles west of Tahiti, at 16°30" South and 151°45" West, Bora Bora is distinctively recognizable by the shape of Mount Temanu, rising above the blue Pacific 2349 feet. James A. Michener, author of *South Pacific* and many other famous books, wrote of Bora Bora as being the most beautiful island in the world. He had traveled the world extensively.

Although the total land mass is only about six square miles, the coral reef surrounding it encompasses a gigantic lagoon, which makes a harbor for even large ships. The crystal-clear waters and colorful coral gardens make for wonderful diving and snorkeling.

Bora Bora, part of the Society Islands, was discovered by Captain Samuel Wallis, on the H. M. S. *Dolphin*, in 1767, and was visited the same year by Captain James Cook (probably the greatest Pacific explorer). The Society Islands became a French protectorate in 1842. A United States Naval and Air base was established on Bora Bora during the Second World War; consequently, many of the Polynesians speak English fluently.

The airport is on a motu, or small island, at the north end of the lagoon, with boat service to the main island. There is also a hotel right next to the airport, but guests who stay there must take a boat trip if they wish to go to any attraction on the main island, which has most of the population, towns, restaurants, and hotels, including the main quay.

The Bora Bora Hotel, situated at the southern end of the lagoon, is a beautiful place, with bungalows on the land, as well as right over the water. The coral gardens just off the Bora Bora Hotel are spectacular, with colorful coral just under the surface. In places these coral gardens deepen into wide depressions, like a giant aquarium with an unbelievable array of coral--and fish, some of them really large.

We were lucky enough to be anchored off the hotel. As is our custom, we asked for the manager, then asked his permission to use their dock for our dinghy trips ashore. We promised that we would not be a nuisance, or make a noise or do anything to annoy or disturb the hotel guests. He very kindly allowed us the use of the dock. We also enjoyed a few excellent meals in the hotel during our stay in Bora Bora.

In the evening, going ashore for dinner or walks, we would watch giant manta rays swimming back and forth off the end of the hotel dock. The lights at the end of the dock drew plankton and other minute marine organisms, which the manta rays would feed on. These magnificent fish, once called "devil fish" because they looked so dangerous, are actually harmless, feeding only on plankton.

We had been told there were many giant manta rays in an area farther up the lagoon, so we moved *Seahorse* and reanchored in another delightful bay, as directed. Our first dive produced an unforgettable experience for my son Steven and me. With scuba gear, we were about thirty feet down when a giant manta ray came slowly towards us. It looked like a B1 bomber, it was so huge. I would guess it spanned over eight feet, wingtip to wingtip. The wing scoops on each side of its mouth encircled a gaping hole big enough for a person to swim into.

It came from the right side of us, and Steve was on my right side. When he was five or six years old, upon seeing a large fish or school of barracuda, he would immediately get on my back until the apparent danger was passed. Now, as the giant manta ray slowed up right in front of us, I thought it was listening to the pounding of my heart, which I'm sure was audible all over the lagoon.

Steven, then seventeen years old, moved closer to it and gently took hold of its wingtip with both hands, holding on until it slowly swam away. We renamed that area Ray Bay. I will never forget the thrill of being so close to such a magnificent fish.

I feel that Mr. Michener knew what he was talking about: Bora Bora is an unforgettable island to visit, well worth the time and effort to get there.

Aitutaki, Cook Islands   13

Heading west from the Society Islands, the next group of islands one comes to is the Cooks. Named for their discoverer, Captain James Cook, they were under British protection from 1888 'till 1901, when the group was included in New Zealand territory.

There are about fifteen small islands stretching from Penryn at eight degrees south latitude, down to Rarotonga at twenty-three degrees south latitude. They are approximately one hundred sixty degrees west longitude. Rarotonga is the main entering port, but it is possible to enter the Cooks at Aitutaki, a northern island of the group. The southern islands are richly forested, while the northern islands are coral atolls.

The population is mostly Polynesian, though all are citizens of New Zealand. Their principal exports are fruit juices, canned pineapple, copra (dried coconut meat), and clothing. Most of these products are sent to New Zealand.

We entered at Aitutaki, anchoring off the island. Though Aitutaki has a beautiful lagoon, the entrance and channel in, has a maximum depth of six feet at high tide. I had wondered, as we approached the island, if we should try to make our way into the lagoon and enjoy the still, crystal-clear water, but our minds were made up when we saw a ketch stuck hard aground halfway in the channel. We anchored in the lee of the island and flew the yellow quarantine flag. When we had no response to our radio calls and saw no launch coming our way, we ventured in by dinghy.

The authorities were most friendly; in fact, as we stepped ashore, a young Polynesian girl came down the quay on a motor scooter and asked us to get on the back for the short ride up to the small government building. My crewman, in his midseventies, was happy to have the ride, especially when she told him to hold tight around her waist with both arms. I was happy to walk, after having been on the boat for four days.

Aitutaki was a quiet, peaceful place, with even the motor scooters just puttering around--even the ones ridden by young people moved along slowly. I couldn't figure how the adults kept the young riders from ripping and roaring around. It was as though all the vehicles had governors fitted to their engines, making it impossible for them to go fast.

The people were extremely friendly; even the authorities could not have been nicer to deal with. We met and talked to a few different New Zealanders who were now living permanently in Aitutaki. They spoke very highly of the quality of life in the Cook Islands. They claimed that there was almost no crime at all in these peaceful islands.

Aitutaki was a delightful stopover on our way west, and checking out was easily accomplished, with the government officials helpful and smiling the whole time.

FIJI 14

We were fortunate to be able to spend some time in Fiji during the delivery of a 46-foot ketch from Papeete, Tahiti, to New Zealand. I had seen many articles and photos of the waters and islands of Fiji, and was looking forward to experiencing it firsthand.

We arrived off the main island, Viti Levu, about one A.M. on a pitch-dark night. Without a moon, we approached the port of Suva cautiously. I had programmed into the GPS the course to the entrance to Suva harbor, also courses right into the harbor, all the way to the center of the anchorage. Since the GPS was coupled to the radar, the radar screen showed the course line with the little circle at the end of the line, where I would change course for a bend in the channel, then the circle representing the spot where we wanted to anchor.

According to the chart, there is a range light system to show the center of the channel into Suva, but neither I nor my 75-year-old crewman could see any range lights, maybe because of all the city lights. Usually I would never enter a strange port after dark unless the range lights were visible and unequivocal. However, the sea was very calm and the wind light, so we slowly ventured in where the GPS and radar said the channel was. As luck would have it, we had entered a strange harbor in the dead of night, moved all the way up a channel with a couple of dog legs, anchored, gone to sleep, and next morning, discovered we were anchored right in the center of the designated anchorage.

We cleared our arrival with the immigration office. The customs officers had come to the boat, and soon all the paperwork was in order, allowing us to cruise all the Fijian islands. We then anchored off the Royal Suva Yacht Club. They were extremely helpful and made us feel very welcome, allowing us to use the club dock for tying up our dinghy, making it easy for us to come and go.

The city of Suva is a bustling, busy metropolis, with every kind of business imaginable. Shops like bazaars, one on top of the other, displayed bargains galore, with many people shopping. There seemed to us to be a lot of hustle and bustle, which made a great deal of noise.

Taxi fares are very reasonable, and taxis are everywhere. We had walked from the yacht club to town for groceries, about a twenty-minute walk. The sun shone hot, and we wondered about the same walk back, carrying bags of food and supplies. As we stepped out of the supermarket, a taxi driver asked us if we needed a cab. I asked how much it would cost to take us to the Suva yacht club, and he replied, "One dollar and a half." With the Fiji rate of exchange in 1993 this was one dollar U.S.

We gladly boarded the taxi, and found the Indian driver a delight. We even booked him in advance for a tour of the area, which took almost a full day. Cost: around thirty dollars U.S. I must add that our driver asked us if he could take us to his home for tea, since his home was on our route. We accepted and were treated to tea and cookies by his wife, dressed in the most beautiful dress or sari. Though she spoke almost no English, she was extremely friendly and a very elegant Indian lady.

They still have firewalkers in Fiji; we attended a firewalking to see how they did it. However, neither of us was very impressed with the show. It was raining––not heavily, but enough to cool the rocks, especially since they scattered and moved the rocks around while they chanted and sang, taking quite a while before venturing onto the rocks. I had seen movie film of firewalking in which they walked on the rocks, with the fire still burning all around. The Fijian firewalkers had put the fire out first, then moved the rocks around for too long. It was a little disappointing.

The education system in Fiji appears to be excellent, with colleges and universities everywhere. Education is mostly free, except for higher levels of studies, which have fees for those who can afford to pay. Literacy is very high: Over 90 percent of men and 80 percent of women can read and write. This is a much higher literacy rate than we have in the U.S.A. The language is English, but I'm sure that almost all can speak Fijian or Indian as well as English. The population is about 50/50 Fijian/Indian.

We sailed from Suva around the south of the island to Nadi (pronounced Nandi), anchoring just off the Fiji Regent Hotel. Close by is also a large Marriot Hotel.

Within one hour of our getting the anchor set, a launch motored out to us. The driver chatted for a while, welcomed us, and gave us a paper of directions showing where we could beach our dinghy, where we could find the laundry rooms, and so forth. We were asked not to beach our dinghy right in front of the hotels, but the space between the two hotels was for boats to use.

A road from the main highway services the beach area between the hotels, bringing people to the charter boats that operate from that area. We were told that it was safe to leave our dinghy unattended, even overnight, in the space between the hotels, as the area was guarded. This was hard to believe, since there were many people coming and going by way of the spare ground between the hotels. Later when we took a taxi back to Suva for two days, we left our dinghy, with outboard motor, gas tank, oars, small anchor and line, et cetera. When we returned, everything was as we had left it.

It was a delightful stay for us off the Fiji Regent Hotel. One of the most enjoyable things was breakfast at the hotel restaurant, overlooking the ocean, ordering coffee and a "bakery basket." This was a large woven tray full of the most delicious assorted bread rolls, scones, and other fresh bakery treats. One bakery basket was more than ample for the two of us, and the prices were most reasonable.

Every evening, sundown was heralded by two burly Fijians beating on a large hollowed-out log drum. The drum was set up by the beach, and as the sound carried through the hotel grounds, a young Fijian man ran all around the area with a flame torch, lighting the many outdoor torch lanterns which were set up on poles.

A short sail from Nadi is Plantation Island, with hotel resorts and the famous Musket Cove Resort. Cruise boats leave the Fiji Regent Hotel area every day for four-hour trips to Plantation Island, stopping at all the hotels, either taking people there for a stay or bringing back vacationers at the end of their stay. There are other charter boats operating from the same area, for longer trips.

A little farther west from Nadi is a group of islands called the Yasawa Group. We were informed that they made a delightful cruising ground, but unfortunately our time was running out, so we had to forego exploring them. The end of September was approaching fast and we needed to head for New Zealand before cyclone season set in.

Fiji is about thirteen hundred miles north of New Zealand and approximately thirty-one hundred miles southwest of Hawaii, on the borderline of Melanesia. Fiji encompasses approximately three hundred islands, the largest of which is Viti Levu, about one hundred miles long, east to west, and roughly sixty miles north to south.

Fiji was under British rule as a colony since 1874, becoming an independent colony in 1970. After two military coups d' etat in 1987, Fiji became an independent republic. At that time the population was half Fijian/Melanesian and half Indian, descendants of migrant workers brought from India while it was a British colony, to work in the sugar cane fields.

The new government is strictly for the benefit of the Fijian/ Melanesians, with all land being reserved for them. It is not allowed for an Indian or any other person to own land. Most businesses were owned and operated by Indians, but after the present government took control, many Indian people left Fiji, feeling they had little future there.

The Fijians tend to live in small clusters of homes, like little villages here and there, while the Indians live in separate homes, most with railings and gates around them. Possibly there is some fear on the part of the Indian population, not having many rights, even though they have lived there for many years and work very hard. We found both the Fijians and the Indian people extremely friendly and helpful.

The climate is tropical, being just eighteen degrees south of the equator. Their winter is the best time, with temperatures between sixty-five and seventy-five degrees, April to October. The summer is hotter, ranging from eighty-five to ninety-five degrees, November through March, with high humidity. Even cyclones are common during summer.

When a sailboat is set up on the ground during the summer, they usually dig a great hole for the keel to fit down into, to make it safer during hurricanes, or cyclones, as they call them.

The highest mountain in Fiji is Mount Victoria, at four thousand six hundred feet.

The main produce is sugar, grown almost everywhere, with little narrow-gauge railway trains running every which way around the island, carrying sugar cane.

Fiji also has a very healthy tourist trade. Most visitors arrive at Nadi (pronounced Nandi) international airport on the western end of Viti Levu.

We couldn't find fault with either the Fijian or the Indian people—all are extremely friendly. The islands are beautiful. The water is crystal-clear. The diving is superb. We will always have happy memories of Fiji.

NEW ZEALAND

All good things come to an end. It was September, and our stay in Fiji was over. My wife had to return to the U.S; her leave of absence had run out.

I cleared customs and immigration easily, fueled up, had enough groceries aboard, and with the weather deteriorating and the early morning actually getting darker, I left Fiji, fearful that a cyclone was developing.

The first day I motor-sailed with a double-reefed mainsail, most of the genoa rolled up, and the mizzen still tied on the boom. The wind rose 'till it blew a steady forty-five miles per hour, naturally coming directly from New Zealand, true to Murphy's Law. At times the yacht moved through the water at only one knot, even with the 85-horsepower diesel working hard. The wind stayed under fifty miles per hour, but the seas were so short and steep, the ketch just couldn't get started making headway before it was slammed on the bow by another big wave, stopping it in its tracks. The first day's run was a disappointing sixty-three miles, noon to noon. *Windrift* usually lopped off one hundred twenty to one hundred and fifty miles a day.

A cyclone did not develop, but the wind remained the same for the next three days, though the wind direction gradually eased around to a more westerly breeze, allowing me to get more sail up. With this, each day's run improved.

During the third day out of Fiji, I stepped down into the main cabin and thought the cabin sole looked extremely glossy. I discovered to my horror that there was water all over the forward part of the cabin floor. One forward floor hatch was floating, though still in its place.

The forward section of the boat did not have a bilge pump

installed, but had scupper holes for water to drain back into the engine room. I guessed that the scupper drain holes were blocked with something, not allowing the water to run back to the engine bilge, where the automatic pump was located. I had not yet figured where the water was coming from.

I immediately rigged up a spare electric pump, to suck from the forward section and pump it into the cockpit, since the hose was not long enough to reach over the side. The pump worked fine; I felt I had everything under control, except that I still did not know where the water had come from. I remembered the owner saying that when the boat was sailing with the rails awash, in heavy seas, there was a leak at the deck/hull joint. I lifted the engine-room hatch to check the bilge, which had not had any water in it before; now there was water running down the inside of the hull like a waterfall.

Now I was really concerned, and started figuring how far I was from the nearest land--still Fiji, probably over two hundred and fifty miles north. I was fearful that the ferrocement hull, though heavily built and with many ocean crossings to its credit, was cracking up in the heavy seas.

I crawled in around the engine room to find the leaks, sweating, worrying, and talking to myself, only to discover water pouring in through a small inspection hatch in the cockpit floor, installed by the manufacturer to facilitate cleaning fuel filters. The emergency pump I had rigged up to drain the forward section, was draining into the cockpit right above the inspection hatch, pouring through onto the fuel tank, and running onto the hull side, flowing down like a wide waterfall. Theoretically I had been pumping the forward section of the boat not overboard, but into the middle section of the boat.

Extending the bilge pump hose moved the flow to over the side, and the waterfall tapered off to nothing. There was a slight leak at the deck line, which had created the flooding in the first place, but now I knew to pump the forward section occasionally.

I was so relieved to learn that the boat was not sinking from under me. A good friend of mine who had served in the U.S. Navy used to say, " A sinking ship at sea can ruin your whole afternoon." He loved understatements.

The fourth day the weather improved, and the wind dropped to around ten mph. The seas calmed and life became good again. I sailed along at five and a half knots, enjoying good food and pleasant sailing; the stereo was playing and all was right with the world. Occasionally a visiting school of dolphins brightened up the scene, and I noticed lots of small jellyfish in the water, becoming more plentiful all the time. I sailed through millions of jellyfish, everywhere, every hour for four days. The water was completely speckled with them, making me wonder just how plentiful they are in the world, and what purpose they serve.

Almost always, sailing the lonely oceans, a boat is followed by one or two albatross. They are a fantastic bird that I believe goes to sea for about seven years. They are expert at riding the wind currents, gliding just over the waves. Sometimes a drooped wingtip touches the water, but they continue to glide; it seems they can go for miles without beating their wings. Their wingspan can reach five feet, so they have a lot of lift and fly very effortlessly. If they land, which I have seen them do occasionally to inspect garbage thrown overboard, they have to run like mad to get airborne again.

The rest of the trip was fairly pleasant, with reasonably good sailing, the weather and sea fairly calm.

The ninth day dawned with my closing on Great Barrier Island, a large island north of Auckland about fifty miles. Because I was getting near land, I had been up watching for any lights most of the previous night, so about seven A.M., being exhausted, I pulled into a small cove in Great Barrier Island, called Nagle Cove, a most delightful place to anchor.

The luscious green rolling hills had many sheep grazing, bleating and calling back and forth to each other. Their sounds and the occasional barking of a dog, coupled with the bay water as calm as glass, all made Nagle Cove a magical place to rest up.

I first made myself a complete breakfast of bacon and eggs, toast, honey, and hot coffee. I then tidied up *Windrift*, washed everything down, then fell into the bunk and slept for about fourteen hours. When crossing an ocean as captain of a small boat, especially if single handing, it is difficult to get a good night's sleep, since you always hear every sound made by the sails or the hull. I'm sure it is like a mother with a new baby, hearing every little sound it makes, and never getting into a sound sleep.

The following morning I hauled anchor, and sadly leaving beautiful Nagle Cove, I headed for Auckland, to check into New Zealand. Right off the city of Auckland I found a large area with boats tied to buoys, with many buoys free. I temporarily tied up and using the VHF radio, called the authorities for instructions.

A voice came right back asking my position. Upon learning I was already in Auckland, he started reading me the riot act for entering New Zealand waters without first getting permission from the proper authorities. He informed me to immediately proceed to the Admiralty Steps, tie up and wait on board. In no way was I to set foot on land without permission. This I did, with my yellow quarantine flag still flying from the starboard spreaders, which I had hauled up before I entered Nagle Cove.

The Admiralty Steps are actually concrete quays, with no wood fender boards to help prevent damage to a hull. There was quite a lot of surge, so I put four large fenders alongside and hoped the ferrocement hull would survive the bumping it was getting.

Very shortly, officials arrived and checked everything. *Windrift* had been built in Auckland some twenty-five years before, and was still registered as a New Zealand vessel. However, this fact did nothing to soften the officious nature of my reception in New Zealand. (Incidentally, I have a British passport as well as my U.S Passport. I had expected better treatment from a colony of Great Britain.)

The time was now around four-thirty, and I had already prepared a salad for my dinner and had set out a hamburger patty to defrost, also a potato and some vegetables. However, the customs official was going through the refrigerator and freezer, also all the food lockers, pulling out all kinds of food and putting them in plastic bags for removal. He even took new blocks of cheese still plastic-wrapped, product of New Zealand, bought in Fiji. He said, "You can't bring any foodstuffs into the country." I pointed out that the cheese had been processed in this same country and the seal was not broken. He took it anyway.

When he had gathered up bags of everything except canned goods, he proceeded to pick up the salad, the hamburger patty, the potato, and the vegetables. I exclaimed that that was my dinner half prepared, which I was going to eat immediately they left. I did not have the dinghy blown up, so I couldn't go ashore for dinner.

I practically begged him to be reasonable, but he picked everything up with a smile on his face, putting everything in separate plastic bags. I had great difficulty keeping my temper under control.

Why would he separate everything carefully, if they were going to incinerate everything as he claimed?

When the Customs "gentleman" (I could use other words better to describe him) left, I was then grilled by the Immigration Officer, who again regaled me for not calling in on VHF radio before entering their waters.

I explained that this was the first time I had ever had a problem, and I had sailed into many foreign ports. And this was a New Zealand registered yacht. When I am going to visit any country by boat, I read everything I can get on the subject; however, I had never heard or seen anything written about this New Zealand law.

He then insisted on reading every entry in my logbook since I left Tahiti. He also wanted the chart showing my daily positions marked. He almost had a heart attack when he understood I had spent the night in Nagle Cove.

Had I contacted anyone ashore? (Of course not.)

Had I gone ashore? (Of course not.)

What did I do there? (Sleep.)

I asked if he had ever crossed an ocean alone. Did he know just how tired a single-hander gets, especially when nearing land?

It took him quite a while to cool off, and I was almost starting to fear that I would be put in jail.

I found New Zealand to be a beautiful country, and the people were very friendly, maybe because I was on a boat. There are more sailboats per capita in New Zealand, than any other place on earth. I am sure of this. I enjoyed a short stay there before flying back to San Francisco, but my impression of their welcoming officials? They were the most obnoxious I have ever encountered.

Now they have devised new laws whereby they can and do examine every yacht wishing to leave N.Z. They will not let you put to sea without all the safety equipment that they insist on, and everything must be in tiptop shape--meaning that it can be even more difficult getting out of N.Z. than it is getting in. This can put a real burden on many cruisers who are sailing on a very tight budget.

It would be my guess that in the future, many boats will go to other countries rather than New Zealand if it is at all possible. I know that this will certainly be the case for me.

HURRICANE 16

This chapter was written not to conjure up thoughts of fun, but to show that even when Mother Nature turns really nasty, small sailing vessels survive, even if it is most uncomfortable for the crew.

JANUARY, 1985: HILO, HAWAII

During a rest and recreation stopover en route from the South Pacific to San Francisco, I met and had dinner with one of the captains of the cruise ships that take passengers around the different Hawaiian Islands. When he heard we were leaving shortly to sail to California, he shuddered, saying, "I wouldn't sail to California in January, not for a million dollars. You will have nothing but gale after gale, the whole way."

I was a little disconcerted, but unfortunately, the cruising insurance coverage on *Seahorse 2* would expire February 20th. I was anxious to reach the mainland before then.

Usually, when planning a trip, I don't bother to check with a weather service, asking for future predictions. I figure that sailboats move slowly across an ocean, usually not much more than one hundred and fifty miles a day. With slow progress like this, it's not possible to get out of the way of a storm or run away from one.

However, with the captain's words ringing in my ears, I rode my folding bike about five miles to the airport, visiting the weather service office located there.

I informed the man on duty of our sailing plans. He was very helpful, and going along a row of machines, he pulled off pages of computer printouts.

After studying them for a short time, he said, "You are very lucky; the Pacific High is really in lower latitudes right now. You should have favorable winds, probably from the northwest, allowing you to hold a course direct to San Francisco."

I was extremely happy to hear the good news. When I had made the same trip in October of 1973, the high-pressure area, covering hundreds of square miles, was lying right between Hawaii and California. At that time, according to the sailing directions, I should sail due north from Hilo until reaching 40 degrees north latitude, then head for San Francisco. I had cut the corner too fine, and sailed right into the high-pressure area.

With no wind whatsoever, the seas became as smooth as glass, and we had to motor, night and day, for eleven days. It was a beautiful portion of the trip. Luckily *Seahorse* carried almost one thousand gallons of diesel fuel.

A few days later two friends of mine arrived in Hilo, from San Francisco; they were going to crew for the trip. Glenn was a retired U. S. Coast Guard officer, and Dave, a man I'd known since he was a little boy. Dave was happy to be adding sea time to his 500-ton captain's license, as he worked toward an upgrade.

With fuel and stores on board, we left Hilo on a beautiful sunny morning, heading for San Francisco in a light southeasterly breeze. We expected to get into the northwesterly wind after we were well clear of the islands. The breeze continued from the southeast the rest of the day.

During the night the wind freshened and came round more easterly, and we hardened in the sails, still keeping almost to our course direct to San Francisco. All the next day the weather continued the same; so much for the northwest winds predicted. However, we were making 125 miles and more each day, beating, with the sails close-hauled.

The automatic pilot steered flawlessly night and day. We ran the engine one hour in the morning, at the same time cooking breakfast. We ran it again for a half-hour around noontime, then again for one hour before sundown, when dinner was cooked. This daily ritual kept the freezer at the correct temperature, the refrigerator cool, and the batteries charged enough to allow the continuous use of the autopilot and other gear.

The third day brought a storm with winds in excess of fifty miles per hour, coming from almost due north. We had to bear off slightly to starboard, heading more easterly. The gale lasted two days, the wind rising to sixty miles per hour at times, before tapering off till it seemed calm with only thirty-miles-per-hour winds.

The wind again veered around until it was blowing from south-southeast. We tacked back onto our original course. We then had two fine days, and hoped the worst was over.

During the trip Dave cooked most of the breakfasts, doing a fantastic job. Glenn, able to turn out the finest dinners, was the prescribed chef for evening meals. The watch system was simple: Each of us had six hours off and three hours on.

Occasionally I heard squeaking from the steering system under the aft cabin berth, though the autopilot was working fine, steering us right on course. The second gale veered the wind back to north, forcing another tack over to starboard, and brought squally, rainy weather for another two days. The squeaking from the steering system became more frequent, but the pilot kept *Seahorse* on course.

I resolved to look for the problem as soon as the weather improved. The gale, again with winds up to sixty miles per hour, had created fairly lumpy seas that would make it more difficult to work on the steering.

The weather again eased up and gave us another two fairly pleasant days. The wind had again returned to south-southeast. I was starting to think that maybe the prediction made by the cruise ship's captain was more correct than that made by the weather service.

By now, twelve days out of Hilo, we were tired of the continuous changes in the weather, though we were glad of the couple of fairly decent days in between storms. The good days, however, were not calm enough or long enough to allow the seas to calm down; consequently, the ocean waves were slowly becoming larger.

I had been putting off working on the steering, but the squeaking was becoming squealing and getting louder, so with the wind still blowing about thirty miles per hour, we started to pull the steering apart.

Seahorse had an emergency tiller that could be fastened to the rudder shaft to steer, once the mechanical steering system was disconnected.   However, someone must steer the boat from his position standing in the aft cabin, with someone else sitting up on the helmsman's seat watching the compass and calling directions down to the one handling the tiller, "Go right, go left."   Glenn sat at the compass, Dave worked the seven-foot tiller, while I dismantled the steering.

When *Seahorse* was being built, I had bought two identical heavy-duty steering boxes, including steering arms already installed on the boxes. This would make it easier to change the complete steering box, in case the change had to be made on the high seas.

Inspection of the now-squealing steering box showed that the position in which the box had to be installed in the boat would not allow the gear oil inside the box to lubricate the sector shaft. This shaft was almost seized-up in the bearing.

Though we were still sailing on course with the yacht's movement fairly erratic, removing the steering and installing the new steering box was accomplished in about one hour with all of us working hard--especially Dave, who, struggling with the tiller, kept us going towards San Francisco. We had lost very little time.

Dave was greatly relieved to get the automatic pilot turned back on and working again.

The wind eased off during the night, and again blew gently from the south-southeast. However, the dawn sky was darker than usual, with heavy cloud cover. The sun was not visible at all. The wind, which had been about eighteen miles per hour, calmed further, to about ten, still from the south-southeast, but great dark clouds formed in stripes across the sky, all the stripes converging towards one spot, to the southeast of our position.

As the day wore on, the cloud formations grew darker, with the same stripe pattern in the sky, all stripes converging to the southeast.

I had taken classes in meteorology a number of times, but could not remember ever hearing about this type of cloud system, though I felt that it did not look good. At four-o clock in the afternoon, already almost dark, it did not look good at all.

At sea, as evening approaches, I always feel a little uneasy, knowing we have hours of charging through the darkness before daylight comes again. In preparation for what looked like nasty weather coming, we shortened sail from the usual working sail area of approximately 1400 square feet, down to the inner storm jib, now giving us only 200 square feet of working sail. With the engine running, we thus motor sailed, still on course for San Francisco.

Around midnight the anemometer needle started to climb, and hour by hour the weather worsened, until by dawn the needle was indicating wind speed of eighty miles per hour, occasionally eighty-five. The sky stayed almost dark all day, with no sun visible. So far, nothing had come apart, we were not taking on any water, and we were still making six to seven knots towards San Francisco.

I think all three of us prayed that it would not get any worse. Unfortunately, if the wind keeps blowing, it stirs up the sea and the waves get bigger and bigger.

Dave said, "Cheer up, things could be worse." I cheered up and sure enough, things got worse!

The wind was continually veering around to south. The seas continued to build.

After fourteen hours of the steady eighty-miles-per-hour wind, the waves were bearing down on us, from our starboard side, higher than our mainmast upper spreaders, which were twenty-seven feet above the deck. Glenn, an experienced Coast Guard officer, estimated them to be at least thirty feet from trough to crest, and the worst he had ever seen.

Although it was not raining, there was so much water in the air from the spindrift—the result of a wave's being blown off sideways— it was blinding to be out in the weather. We were happy to have a partially enclosed deckhouse that sheltered us quite a lot.

Seahorse continued to rise to each wave, but as the wind continued, occasionally a larger wave would break before it reached us, and it was like being in the surf. We were still motor sailing, with the autopilot working tirelessly, trying to keep us on some semblance of a course.

We continued to keep watches, though the visibility was almost zero; the watch person had to tie himself to the helm seat, the movement of the yacht was so violent. When every second or third wave broke, we were knocked down, time after time. So much water came over the boat that green water filled the sail also, pushing the yacht over until the water spilled out of the sail. Each time a breaking wave hit, it pushed the whole boat sideways in the white foam at least fifty feet before *Seahorse* righted herself and sailed on.

I had the aft cabin, which had a large double berth athwartships (across the beam of the boat, so, when sailing, you sleep or lie in the berth with your feet to the low side). When *Seahorse* got knocked down, I'd find myself, with the berth vertical, standing on the locker door at the end of the berth, knowing that the masts must be almost lying on the water, wondering if she was going to come back up. She always did!

During the afternoon, after a very violent knockdown, there was a strong smell of hot or burning diesel fuel from the engine room. Quickly opening the engine room hatch, we saw diesel fuel spilling all over the hot engine.

We immediately shut down the engine. Further inspection revealed that a heavy, spare, stainless steel line shaft about thirty inches long and one and a quarter inches in diameter, which had been stored in the engine room (wedged behind a large steel toolbox and the hull), had rolled over the box during the last knockdown, smashing across the top of the engine.

During its flight across the engine, the loose line shaft had smashed the fuel return line, a small copper pipe, right off its fitting, leaving diesel fuel spilling out. We were so lucky the engine was not so hot as to start a fire.

Though I have never experienced it, I know for sure, from common sense, that a fire at sea, a thousand miles from land, could ruin your whole afternoon.

Now, with the motor off, and not knowing how or when we might be able to repair the damaged copper line, we had to switch the automatic pilot off and hand-steer. Just what we needed: more work for an already exhausted crew!

With no motor, we had neither battery charging nor electricity, so we had to conserve the batteries.

The mainmast, where the inner jib stay head is fitted, should have been fitted with running back stays to counteract the pull of the inner jib in heavy weather. These stays had been considered unnecessary, since the mainmast was very heavy-duty.

To see how the mast was faring, I crawled up on deck, with my safety harness securely holding me to the boat. Going over the side in this maelstrom would certainly have been my last swim.

On the deck at the foot of the mainmast, looking up at the masthead, I was horrified to see the center of the mast shaking back and forward, moving about two feet each way.

When *Seahorse* was down in the trough of the wave, there was almost no wind. Then rising up the next wave, the wind would shriek through the rigging, making noise like a thousand demons, shaking the mast unbelievably. The shaking was felt throughout the boat, until we rose up the next wave and the sail got the blast of wind, which steadied things for a short time. The next cycle would continue, creating the awful shaking of the whole rigging.

I wondered how long the Sitka spruce mast could take this kind of punishment. I'm certain an aluminum mast would already have been lost over the side because of metal fatigue.

As the wind was continuing to veer around clockwise on the compass, we knew we were going to be forced to jibe the inner jib, which was loose fitted to a boom. With no motor to help swing *Seahorse* around, I was concerned that an uncontrolled jibe could send the whole rig overboard, leaving us with neither sailing ability nor motor, and the wind still blowing eighty plus miles per hour.

We were still making the course towards San Francisco, averaging about seven knots. This was about half a knot up the waves and up to twelve knots on the downside. What a ride: *Seahorse* had never before moved so fast through the water as she did surfing down those waves.

It finally came time to jibe, and the act I had been dreading was so easily accomplished, I could hardly believe it. When *Seahorse* ran down to the bottom of a wave and was completely in the trough with no wind, I wheeled her over, the boom swung over with the sail, and we were easily ready for the next blast when we rose up again into the wind.

After almost twenty hours of eighty-plus miles per hour winds veering around the compass until the blow was coming from west, then the northwest, the wind finally settled from the north. The indicator needle of the anemometer started gradually to show a decrease in the velocity.

The barometer, which had dropped before the hurricane began— though not as much as I thought it should have dropped, considering the weather we got—was gradually rising. The sky was becoming lighter by the hour. We figured the worst was over. However, we were still hand steering, and all three of us were extremely tired.

It was the third day since we had shut the motor down when the seas, though still enormous, had calmed enough to allow working on the motor. The seas were still very lumpy, and the yacht's motion was still anything but smooth, but we decided that we had to tackle the problem anyway.

During the nighttime, we had to show navigation lights, and everyday living uses battery power. I was concerned about the house batteries being so low that if we needed them coupled to the engine start battery, they would not be any help when it came time to get the engine started.

We had on board a small 400-watt gasoline generator made by Honda. This is not a lot of 120-volt power, but in an emergency it could help do some things.

In the toolbox were two electric soldering guns. The first one I checked needed 750 watts. My heart sank. I feared that both guns used the same amount of power; however, the second gun's little nameplate showed it required only 375 watts.

Then the question was, could a low-power solder gun generate enough heat to properly solder the small copper pipe to the fairly heavy copper fitting it had been ripped from?

From the engine we removed the complete return line pipe and the end part, and we cleaned both parts to be soldered. With the Honda generator running, Glenn steered *Seahorse*, Dave held the fittings together, and I held the solder gun tip against them.

I don't know how long we held this position; I know both Dave and I were cramped, with arms aching, but we couldn't let the soldering tip move away from the pipe and fitting until they heated up enough for the solder to flow.

Eventually we could see a little melting of the solder, and slowly, so slowly, we gradually built up quite a lot of solder all around the complete fittings. Now, as long as it didn't leak . . . .

It did not take too long to reinstall the return line along the top of the engine, and soon we were ready to fire it up. The first touch of the starter button, however, moved the crankshaft only about one-eighth of a revolution. I thought the engine start battery was dead, but checking the voltmeter, I saw that the reading was 13 volts--almost fully charged--so what was the problem now?

A second try, with the ship's batteries at 11.5 volts coupled with the engine battery, did not move the crankshaft any farther. I feared that the starter motor had died, which usually never happens without showing signs of weakening power over a long period of time.   We had no spare starter motor.

There were holes through the front end of the crankshaft to allow a mechanic to use a pry bar to slowly turn the engine over when timing it, and so forth. We used a bar, and found we could not move the crankshaft at all. This meant that the engine must be hydraulically locked, with water or fuel filled into the cylinders, preventing the pistons from rising in the cylinders--very depressing news.

"What did you say, Dave, about cheering up?"

What can you do but keep on working?

We removed all the cylinder injectors; one feeds each cylinder. With the bar, we turned the crankshaft, which gushed water out of two of the cylinders. Checking the water by taste proved it to be salt water.

We could only think that the exhaust system had been completely back-flooded by the knockdowns after we had shut down the engine. Had the engine been able to keeep operating, it would have kept the exhaust clear.

With all water removed from the cylinders, the injectors were reinstalled, everything was connected, and we were ready to try to start the engine again, hoping that the salt water had not destroyed the pistons, rings, or any other interior parts. In case the salt water had seeped down into the lubricating oil, we changed the engine oil and oil filter.

The starter motor now turned the engine over, though a little slower than usual, but did not fire the engine.

I pressed the "jet start" button, a system that gives each cylinder a shot of ether, and the diesel fired but stopped immediately. We repeated the attempt to start, touching again the ether button, and lo and behold, after two or three shots of ether it fired up and purred like a kitten.

I ran it for a matter of minutes, and the engine sounded fine, so I called up to Dave, who had been hand steering, "OK Dave, you can turn on the autopilot." To which he replied, "It's on already. I switched it on the second the engine fired."

The relief we all felt from the engine running again made us a little giddy; we laughed at each other or at nothing. Yippee! No more hand steering. We may, for a while, have acted like three drunken sailors. The moderating of the weather system, coupled with the engine running again, especially the automatic pilot steering, eased our lives tremendously.

Although we were all completely exhausted, Glenn prepared the most delicious dinner, with salad, chicken cooked in a white wine sauce, vegetables, et cetera. That evening Dave watched a video movie; though he had seen it a number of times, he seemed to enjoy it more than ever.

With the dissipation of the hurricane, the wind settled in from the north, continuing the same for the rest of the journey, with wind speed holding around twenty-five to thirty-five miles per hour. The last two days before sailing under the Golden Gate Bridge we spent lazing around, happy to have lived through the three gales and one hurricane during the twenty-five hundred miles sailed from Hawaii, with everything and everybody still intact.

This was not the most enjoyable cruise, but it was certainly a very memorable one.

SAILING

Part Three

Making Money
With Your Boat

INTRODUCTION 17

You might be among the lucky few who have a large, secure cruising budget, in which case the following chapters may not be of much interest to you. However, even though we found the cruising life to be very inexpensive, we met many sailors using many ways to make money in the marine field, and I will go over some of these ways in the following chapters.

If you are still just contemplating buying a boat, there are companies like The Moorings who have charter boats in different parts of the world, usually the most beautiful cruising grounds they have found. It is possible to purchase the yacht from them or a similar company. They continue to look after it, service it, and charter it out; chartering may almost make enough money to cover the payments. This is often called Lease-Back Chartering Purchase.

There are restrictions in this system if you are going commercial and writing everything off your income taxes. You may only use the boat a certain number of days or weeks per year, but it could be a nice way to get the boat paid off. Your tax accountant can explain the details of this system as regards the Internal Revenue Service.

The Moorings at times have for sale used boats from their fleet, or they may know of one for sale by an owner who, for one reason or another, now wants to sell. The Moorings telephone number is 1-800-535-7289. They are one of the most reliable charter firms I know of. The company is extremely well organized.

I myself have never had any dealings with The Moorings, but I have different friends who have, and all have had nothing but praise for the way they were treated. The boats were spotlessly clean, well equipped, and comfortable; the stores they had asked for were on board; and everything was shipshape, with all systems working.

One friend reported having trouble on a cruise in French Polynesia. The cooling water pump on the engine was not working. He called the Mooring's office, which was on the island he had left— about four hours' sailing time away. The office manager apologized for the inconvenience, asking them to stay put and promising that they would send a mechanic to fix the problem. In a short time a mechanic arrived and installed a new pump, allowing my friends to continue their charter without losing too much time.

My own experience came from observing the many charterers we met while we were cruising the South Pacific, and talking to them about their experiences. The comments almost always were favorable.

There are charter companies almost every place that there is good sailing. If you already own a boat, check with your local charter companies. Many will enroll your boat in their program, though they sometimes charge a fee for you to join.

The same lease-back system works, and if you charter your boat locally, it enables you to service it yourself and save a little money. You can also take it out for a sail to make sure that all systems are working.

There are lots of boats that sit in their berths too long, without moving. The owners are usually busy with business or other activities. It would be better to have the boats used. This is a way to do it, and the money taken in helps to pay the berth rental and sometimes a lot more.

Best of all, if you have now turned your boat into a commercial venture, you can legally write off the expenses of owning your boat. Every little bit helps when it comes time to do your income taxes. Of course the down side is that you also have to declare any money you receive from chartering your boat.

LOOK FOR THE FREE MONEY   18

Money is available from the U. S. Government for all kinds of projects regarding boating, especially if you have a degree in oceanography, marine biology, or anything to do with the marine field. There are many books in the local library explaining exactly how one goes about procuring a grant. You may have an idea that you want to explore, or have a theory about a particular fish or marine life that you want to study in greater detail.

In the Tuamotu Archipelago I ran across a 50-foot ketch crewed by three men and two girls. They were studying the behavior of sharks and were all living on grant money, which they received each month. I asked them exactly what they had done to obtain their grant and was told that one of the crew, who had a bachelor's degree in oceanography, had made an application and been given the grant. He then found a boat and owner, put together the crew, and off they went to the South Pacific.

They were having a ball, and every few days they would chum the water with chopped-up fish they had caught, tieing a large piece of meat on a line and hanging it over the side. Whatever happened then when a shark came around, they would describe in a written article that they would send to Washington D.C. It appeared that enough money came from the government to pay all the expenses for the whole group to cruise the tropical waters of French Polynesia as though they were on vacation.

Another sailor I met in Tahiti was living on grant money. He was a marine biologist who was studying the reefs and checking out how many Crown of Thorns starfish there were. This was interesting to me, because I had inadvertently touched one of these dangerous starfish, gotten a stinger in my left index finger, and had spent six weeks attending hospital every other day for treatment. The pain was so severe I had considered having the stung finger removed entirely.*

A third gentleman, actually a friend, has lived most of his life on grants from the government. He had a degree in the marine field, and his latest grant supplied enough money to take a group of approximately forty people to the Cook Islands, in the South Pacific. The expedition was formed to find a certain little Japanese snail that had been reported seen in the waters of Suvarov, one of the northern Cook Islands.

The money was available to fly these people from the East Coast of the United States to Raritonga, the main island of the Cooks, then ferry them, six at a time, in a small plane up to the nearest island to Suvarov that had an airstrip, finally chartering a boat to get them to their destination. The grant money supplied all the food and necessary equipment for this venture, all to find a small, insignificant snail.

So it would appear that there is money available, if you can come up with something to study.

Reference books on the subject of government grant money are numerous, and available for scrutiny at your local library. Titles worth seeking are:

Plain Talk About Grants, by Robert E. Geller. Although dealing mostly with the field of rehabilitation, developmental services, and mental health, this collection of material and its concise how-to format may help anyone seeking funding for any project.

The Art of Winning Foundation Grants, and *The Art of Winning Government Grants*, both by Howard Hillman. Mr. Hillman explains in detail how to navigate the maze of government offices to find the matching grant for an individual applicant, and advises how to fill out the complex application forms. He tells how to find the right agency and leads the grant seeker to the possibility of government cash.

How To Write a Winning Proposal, by Virginia Larson. She has many tips on how to write a good proposal and much information on using word processing to assist you in writing a winning proposal.

The Foundation Center's User-Friendly Guide, compiled by Public Staff of the Foundation Center. Editors: Margaret Morth and Sarah

Collins. This book covers foundations in detail. Though dealing mostly with nonprofit organizations, it contains helpful information.

The Action Guide To Government Grants, Loans and Giveaways, by George Chelekis. This is a most comprehensive book of over five hundred pages, explaining the art of getting millions of dollars in grants, loan guarantees, and other financial help from federal and state government sources.

* The Crown of Thorns starfish is a giant disc with five or more arms extending out from the disc or body. It does not really resemble the usual small starfish seen almost everywhere, which are completely harmless. But beware the Crown of Thorns type. It has blunt-appearing spines all over its skin, and though these look blunt, almost resembling the heavy stone spines of a type of sea urchin, in fact they can inject a deadly painful spine into your flesh—even through diving gloves. Whatever it injects into you causes the most intense pain and almost paralyzes the part stung.

The Crown of Thorns starfish do not move, except very slowly. They cling to the reef and devour the coral underneath their body. Measuring up to two feet or more across and sometimes invading a reef in great numbers, they can destroy a vast amount of coral. The marine biologist stated that they had carefully collected a great number of them, ground them up for fertilizer, and had disastrous results. They discovered that nothing would grow in the soil so fertilized.

Another observation supports the toxicity of this species: When you are snorkeling and chop up a sea urchin or clam, the little fish will crowd around you for the free food, but not when you cut into the body of a Crown of Thorns starfish. They will not eat any of it. The meat must be poison even to other fish.

At that time, the marine biologists had not learned of any way to get rid of them. The gentleman I met also said that if you cut off a part of a Crown of Thorns starfish it would grow a complete new full body

from the piece. I mentioned how painful it had been and still was. So
he tried to cheer me up with the statement, "We call the sting from a
Crown of Thorns starfish, the 'eight years of pain sting.'"

It did pain me for many years; in fact, it is still tender, so
even though they do not look dangerous, do not touch one on any
account.

Design and Build Boats   19

Building Boats

Building boats for sale is possible, though it requires an investment in quite a lot of tools and equipment—also a yard, preferably near the water or within launching distance of water. This can also be a long time commitment, which may not be what you are interested in, especially if you have broken away from the humdrum of everyday business life and are living a more free and easy-going life on your boat.

There are, however, many established boat yards around the country where you may find temporary employment for your skills. It is even possible to find a local guy building his own boat who would employ an extra person when the job requires two sets of hands.

Working for a while for a local boat yard can really supplement your cruising kitty, and as I said before, boat yards, especially if they build boats as well as repair them, employ people of many different skills. The larger yards are almost always looking for skilled employees. Even unskilled work is usually available: sanding and grinding boat bottoms, sanding and prepping paintwork, and masking up before spray painting is started. Even sweeping up around the yard is a necessary job that doesn't tax you too much.

Working for a boat yard does not necessitate your having to buy a lot of equipment, and when you are ready to move on, there is nothing tying you down. You can build up your cash and then go cruising for a while longer.

DESIGN CHANGES

Perhaps you are a designer at heart, looking for fulfillment in your life. There are many boats that were built with glaring faults in the original design. Owners change things from time to time, wanting a different sitting arrangement, or larger bed, or separate beds instead of a double bed. If you can sketch out what you would do to improve a cabin layout or make suggestions for a particular addition to a cabin, you may be commissioned to draw up plans for different owners who have always been unhappy with some particulars of their boat.

One of the mistakes many designers often make is cramming the boat with sleeping berths. A designer I once talked to regarding a 48-foot sailboat, claimed he could design it with up to eighteen berths. I didn't even know eighteen people I would like to have sleep over. Unfortunately, designers are often driven by a public who, if they hear you have a boat, invariably ask, "How many does it sleep?"

Boats are often designed to sleep eight or ten persons, yet cannot carry enough food to feed four for an overnight stay. Once an owner realizes this, he or she may wish to rip out some of the berthing, replacing it with more useful storage lockers or drawers, or more comfortable seating arrangements.

There are owners waiting for suggestions.

CONSULTING

There are many people with vast experience at cruising who are capable of advising neophytes who are just getting started in sailing. You may be one of those experienced sailors who could give expert advice and be a consultant.

Beginners don't know what type of boat to buy, what equipment it should have, or even how to go about outfitting a yacht for serious cruising. I have known wealthy beginners who used the services of a consultant for months, even a year or so, until they had everything exactly the way they wanted. The consultant was paid to work with the boat yard during a major refit, which took quite a long time. The consultant's efforts, coupled with many good, common-sense ideas of the owner, created a fine, completely equipped sailing yacht that any sailor would have been proud to own.

Sailing school bulletin boards are a good place to put up your card. It is a place to start, contacting those who are just starting to learn sailing. An advertisement in a local sailing magazine may sell your services. If you are a capable speaker, arrange with a local yacht club for you to give a talk on "boating for beginners." You may find a number of people needing your talents, some willing to pay well for the learning experience of one-to-one instructions.

SELL BOATS 20

YACHT SALES AND BROKERAGE

If you have an easy manner and enjoy meeting people, if you like boats, are happy being around the water, and have time on your hands, why not go into yacht sales?

There are certain state regulations regarding permits and licenses that must be addressed. I was employed as a salesman one year when I had suffered an arm injury and couldn't work at my regular job. To sell new boats, no license was required, though a person had to have a license to sell used boats.

I really enjoyed the experience for almost a year, except that sales were very slow because at that time bank interest rate on loans was around 20 percent, making payments totally out of the question except for the very wealthy. However, lately with interest rates much lower, sales are much better.

When you have a sale pending, there is always a sea trial to perform, to make sure everything works. The autopilot, anchor windlass, quality of engine powering in forward and reverse, the radios, radar, and so forth, must all be checked. This means that you have to go sailing, and these little jaunts add a lot of fun to the job.

It is a good idea to take the prospective boat out before the sea trial day arrives. This will give you a dry run, allowing you to learn the boat's handling capabilities and just generally getting to know the boat and all systems therein. You will be a more competent salesperson, able to show the yacht to the best advantage.

Like most selling occupations, it takes time to make a name for yourself, make contacts, and find out the best way to get clients. Leave your business cards all over the place. You can scan the newspaper ads, yachting magazines, and marine publications checking for leads— boats for sale by owner, boats wanted, and so forth. You may get a listing, even an exclusive listing, guaranteeing you a commission no matter who sells the yacht. Also you have to get to know what boats are available in your area.

When a prospective buyer comes to you, it is necessary to spend time finding out exactly what your clients have in mind. Are the clients experienced? Do they know exactly what type of boat they are looking for? Is this going to be their first boat? Are they looking for suggestions and help in every aspect of buying a boat?

Are they planning long distance sailing, racing, fishing near home? It's up to you to suggest the right type of boat to suit their needs and dreams, then show them any suitable craft available in the neighborhood and hopefully get a deal going.

Once you get rolling and can make a fair living selling boats, it is a fun way to spend your time.

HIRE OUT YOUR BOAT 21

CHARTER YOUR BOAT

One fairly easy way to make money with your boat is to charter it to people who want to be out on the water occasionally. If you don't mind risking your boat with a stranger you can rent it out bare boat, which is without a skipper. For six passengers or fewer you do not have to have the boat licensed by the U. S. Coast Guard, though it must have all the necessary safety equipment on board.

If letting your yacht out with a stranger is more than you can tolerate, you can get your six-pack license (to take six passengers at a time). The tests, given by the Coast Guard, are fairly simple. They cover the rules of the road, safety precautions, emergency procedures the captain must know, and so forth. There is a restriction that you must have been sailing for one year in the area in which you wish to charter. All the necessary facts can be read in literature you can get from the Coast Guard.

There are classes for getting the six-pack license and the instructor's guarantee you will pass the license tests when you finish the course. These classes are advertised in local boating magazines.

After you acquire the six-pack license you can make yourself available to any local charter company. They may use you as a skipper or with your own boat when they are booked up with their own fleet.

Place an advertisement in the local papers or boating circulars. Printing up a brochure explaining your services, including photographs of your boat inside and out, will also help to increase your business, especially if your boat shows well.

If you have a larger yacht, say forty or fifty feet or more and it can pass Coast Guard inspection, you can go for the heavier license. This will allow you to carry more than six paying passengers. The number of passengers you will be licensed to take will be determined by the stability test you must perform for the Coast Guard. This is part of the total safety inspection the Coast Guard will perform on your boat.

The inspection requires you to have extra safety equipment on board and special life preservers, etc., but when you can take out fifteen or fifty passengers or more, the extra revenue you can generate is tremendous. Since there are not so many sailboats with the larger license, the ones that are licensed are in greater demand. You may also cater lunch or dinner for your guests and add to the revenue received for the charter.

Once you are licensed to take passengers for hire, the door is opened for all kinds of exciting, money-making ventures. Many people would love to take sailing lessons, and it is a lot of fun teaching those who are anxious to learn. If you are based on the California coast, there is whale-watching at certain times of the year as the whales migrate north or south to winter or to breed. Depending on your location, there may be other types of sea life for wildlife-watching trips.

I will always remember an experience I had in the Pacific Ocean halfway between Hawaii and San Francisco. Our autopilot had quit, and with only two of us on board, hand steering had us both very tired. On my watch I was standing in the cockpit at the wheel as we sailed easily along in a gentle breeze. I was dozing and nodding off at times, when suddenly I came to my senses with the most awful fishy smell I had ever experienced. I almost panicked at the sight of a large school or pod of humpback whales completely surrounding the boat.

Immediately I remembered stories of whaleboats being attacked, and though *Seahorse* was a heavy steel ketch, I was a little concerned. They were swimming at about six knots to our five, going in the same direction, close alongside.

One whale about forty feet long, no more than ten feet from our beam, surfaced to breathe, then his tail rose high up in the air with the giant tail fins looking like the wings of a small airplane. I expected to be drenched with salt water as he drove his tail, now just ahead of the cockpit, down into the water. However, the whale brought his tail down so gently it didn't make a ripple.

It was quite a while before the whales pulled ahead and left us behind. The encounter left the two of us with the most wonderful memories that I'm sure will stay with me for the remainder of my life.

There are charter companies like Ocean Voyages in Sausalito, California, owned and run by Mary Crowley. Mary and her knowledgeable crew organize all kinds of charters worldwide. Depending on your schedule, and if you can change your departures somewhat, Mary Crowley or some other charter service may be able to set you up with paying passengers for almost anywhere you wish to cruise.

I once met a sailor with a CSY 44 cruising ketch who had just finished a ten-year circumnavigation of the world. During each leg of the trip he carried paying passengers all organized by Mary Crowley. Charters had paid all this sailor's expenses for a round-the-world sail lasting almost ten years, making him many friends and acquaintances in the process.

There may be a market for you to rent your boat without its leaving the berth. It is possible to rent to people who would like to spend a romantic evening on a boat, but who don't feel confident enough to take it out boating. You can rent for the evening, or overnight.

If your boat is berthed near the city and you only use it on weekends, like most owners, the possibility exists for you to find a person or couple anxious to rent a place to sleep near their work. You can rent it as a sleeping place from Sunday night 'till Friday morning. Many people with a long commute to work would be happy to have a place to sleep near their work, then go home for the weekend. This arrangement makes you money but still leaves your boat available to you Friday, Saturday, and Sunday.

Whatever way you make money with your boat, it opens the door to have it as a commercial venture, allowing all kinds of deductions on your income tax.

Talk to your tax adviser.

SCUBA DIVING AND SNORKELING

There is great joy in exploring the undersea world. I'm sure most people have thrilled at watching the movies made by the inventor and world famous diver, Jacques Yves Cousteau. Captain Cousteau and associates invented in 1943 the self-contained underwater breathing apparatus or Scuba, as it is known today. Cousteau continued to spend the rest of his life studying the oceans of the world aboard *Calypso*. He formed undersea laboratories in which divers lived for days at a time, making all kinds of experiments, documenting and photographing undersea life.

Before Scuba gear, the only way for a human to spend time under the water was in a cumbersome, heavy diver's suit with helmet. When using this expensive equipment, it was necessary to have a boat with a large air pump, turned by hand, to pressure pump air down to the diver below. Because of the costs of this type of diving, only commercial ventures used the system.

With the advent of Scuba, diving was brought within the reach of almost anyone. Once the Scuba gear is purchased or rented, it is only a matter of driving to a swimming area and walking into the water until it's deep enough for you to dive and enjoy another world.

Diving with Scuba gear without proper training can be very dangerous, if not fatal. This is an activity for which you need training by a professional. It is necessary to study and attend classes to learn exactly how to dive safely. You must know how to figure the length of time you can stay on the bottom, depending on the depth of the dive, and how long you must wait before it is safe to dive again. Once you understand how to work the dive tables, it is relatively easy to be safe and have wonderful experiences. but diving is not a sport to be taken lightly.

Many people enjoy diving for years and years, but few are careless about the rules. It is prudent to always dive with a partner, since it is possible to share another's air in the event that one diver doesn't notice his air tank is almost empty. This is one of the many things you learn when taking the Scuba lessons to obtain your license.

The first time I went diving was while I was vacationing in Hawaii, many years ago. The hotel had different tours arranged, and one tour was Scuba diving. About ten would-be divers, including myself, were taken out on a sailboat until we were in water approximately forty feet deep. No one had been diving before, so the skipper of the boat, who was the dive master, gave us about a five-minute lesson. He mainly paired us up, two by two, and instructed us to watch each other, and give each other the thumb-and-finger circle as long as all was OK.

It was a nervous group that headed down the anchor chain, heading for the bottom. I was teamed with a boy about ten years of age, and he and I exchanged the OK sign about a hundred times during the twenty minutes the dive lasted. We were reassuring each other and we all survived.

However, since then I have been certified as a PADI ocean diver and the training for this was very involved. I have wondered many times thinking back on that first dive, what would have happened if one or two of us neophytes had panicked at a depth of forty feet. No one had any idea what to do in an emergency, nor did we have any idea how to share our air with a buddy who had run out of air.

Offering diving charters, with your boat being used as the dive platform, can earn you money. You will need to know where the best diving areas are located, and soon you may have steady customers chartering your yacht. Installing a high-pressure compressor on board will enable you to also fill the scuba tanks; this service can extend the diving activities, rather than your having to head home as soon as the tanks are empty.

Of course the captain needs to be licensed by the U. S. Coast Guard to take passengers for hire. If you wish to take more than six paying passengers, the boat also has to be Coast Guard licensed.

You may have some diving accessories for sale, since things like straps break, and small things get lost. Underwater photography equipment may be rented to your passengers. It has been my experience that Scuba divers spend quite a lot of money on equipment, and are always keen to go diving.

If you acquire your instructor's license, you may find it profitable running a training school for Scuba lessons. New people taking up the sport may lead to more people wanting to charter your yacht in the future.

FISHING COMMERCIALLY

I have seen pleasure boats set up for commercial fishing, even though they may not be able to carry large quantities of fish. When prices are good, it can be a way to supplement your budget.

For many years the San Francisco fishing fleet consisted of small, 30-foot Monterey fishing boats that would leave the dock early in the morning and be back in the late afternoon. These boats did not have a very large fish hold, yet many men made their livelihood fishing with this small boat.

Nowadays large fish companies own much larger boats, which need captains and crew. If you are an experienced fisherman or operator, there may be a position for you to captain one of these boats or to crew on them.

There are also party boats operating out of most ports, taking ordinary people out for day fishing. They supply all the necessary gear, and usually can take up to fifty people per trip. These party boats also use paid skippers and crew.

It is required that you have your Coast Guard license to take paying passengers on a boat, whether fishing or not.

BOATING INSTRUCTOR

Once you are experienced at sailing, there is a world of opportunity to give sailing lessons, especially if you have acquired a Coast Guard captain's license.

There is a host of topics relating to boating:

Boat handling

Sailing

Navigation, both coastal and ocean

Piloting along a coast

Celestial navigation using a sextant, tables, and chronometer to find your way across any ocean

Crew-overboard recovery drills

Dinghy handling; outboard motor use

Electronic navigation, using satellite systems, radar, depth sounders, Loran, chart plotters, sonar (a more sophisticated depth sounder), and VHF radio operation

Anchoring, which is a very important aspect of boating

How to avoid mishaps and enjoy the world of boating

You can run schools or classes on any or all of these subjects, mostly using your own boat, and for sailing lessons, small sailing dinghies are best. Students learn sailing faster in a small boat than they do in a larger yacht. The larger yacht will allow a person to make more errors and still be much more forgiving. Things also happen slower in a large sailboat; consequently, the student learns more slowly.

Once a person can handle a small sailing dinghy, he or she will find it easier to control a larger boat. Of course, you cannot sail right into the dock with a large boat--that might demolish the dock, whereas a small dinghy would only bounce off.

Usually a larger yacht will have an engine, making it easier to berth the boat. It is, however, good to practice sailing a boat right into her berth. You should practice this with the engine running, but the gearshift in neutral. In the event of difficulties or misjudgments, the engine can be put into gear to assist your getting the boat into her berth.

Sailing is such fun to teach; not only do you get paid for going sailing, but also the students are usually very keen to learn everything they can about the subject. It is wonderful to see a total beginner gradually become a competent boat handler, confidently taking the controls and maneuvering the boat into and out of a crowded yacht harbor, stopping when necessary, and turning the boat around in its own length and heading out again, completely in control.

If you live in an area where the water is warm enough to swim, you can teach swimming and diving. Countless people who have never learned to swim have the desire to do so. It's a matter of their gaining the confidence to relax in the water. If they persist and learn to swim, they will be so pleased with themselves, and forever thankful that they took the trouble to learn.

Salvaging, Towing, and Vessel Assist

Unfortunately, there are often boats that have a problem. Common is running aground, anchoring too close to shore at high tide and being left high and dry when the tide goes out, or ending up high and dry by being blown ashore by the wind if the motor cannot be started. These types of problems can occur for any number of reasons.

Once you are aground, it's best to wait for high tide. Having a dinghy will allow you to take an anchor out to deep water and set it. Then you may be able to kedge out toward the anchor, pulling your boat off the bottom to deeper water. If you cannot get yourself off at high tide, you will need to be towed off by another vessel in order to save your boat.

Sometimes, through miscalculations you run out of fuel. Maybe there was a high headwind against you when you were returning to port. Maybe you simply forgot to check your fuel tanks. In any case, your boat may need a tow, or someone to bring fuel.

For many years the Coast Guard came to your assistance free of charge, no matter what problem you had, even if the problem was caused by carelessness or stupidity. Now, however, you can be charged for the tow or the help if the officer deems it was simply running out of fuel or some other careless act that caused the problem.

When people go boating, they should be as self-sufficient as possible, making sure that all systems are in good working order. You must check that the total journey planned does not require more fuel than the boat is carrying. You must plan a refueling stop along the way.

A genuine breakdown at some time cannot be avoided, so it is a good idea to belong to an organization like Vessel Assist. These are organizations that operate like AAA: You pay a yearly fee and you will be towed or assisted if the need arises.

You may want to set up your boat for salvaging and towing. In an area where there are many yacht harbors and marinas, there are always unfortunate boaters needing assistance. Especially on a windy, stormy day, things can get out of control very easily. Murphy's Law dictates that problems never arise when everything is calm and pleasant.

Of course, organizing yourself as a towboat necessitates circulating your phone number around boat owners and being available almost anytime. This is made easier nowadays with the availability of cellular phones and their fairly reasonable service.

If you are the courageous type and are scuba experienced, there is always the need for divers to do salvage work. You may be called to refloat a boat, or retrieve equipment from the bottom or from a sunken vessel.

In waters that are cold and murky, this is not a pleasant occupation, though there are many divers who enjoy any kind of activity under water. This kind of activity can be very enjoyable if the water is warm and clear.

Help Them Get Their Boat There 22

Yacht Delivery

If you are not nervous about handling different boats, you may be interested in yacht delivery. Many boat owners cruise to their favorite area and spend as much time as possible there, but when it comes time to return to work or business, they sometimes will hire a skipper to bring their boat home. Depending upon where they finish the cruise, the sail home may be easy or a difficult upwind beat for days or weeks.

There are places in the world where boats just sit, the owner neither wanting to go farther nor desiring to make the more difficult journey home. Mexico is the end of the line for many cruising people; Tahiti is another place, as are Fiji and New Zealand. Then there is also the Mediterranean. Of course, wealthy owners will often pay to have their yachts taken both ways, since many of them have pressures of business that won't allow them to spend the time it takes to cross an ocean.

Yachts can be shipped almost anywhere in the world, but the shipping will usually require the yacht to be set in a sturdy steel frame or cradle that can be set on the deck of a freighter and fastened down firmly. The steel cradle must be very strong, to stand up to a possible storm at sea without buckling or breaking under the weight of the yacht during the extreme conditions which might be encountered on the ocean. Once the steel base with the yacht fastened to it is lifted onto the freighter, the cost of the trip is not so outrageous, but the steel cradle can be very expensive.

When you get a contract to deliver a yacht, there are some details to work out with the owner:

Is the yacht in safe working condition?

Does it have all the necessary safety equipment on board?

Are all bills that may have been accrued in a foreign country paid up to date?

Is there insurance currently on the yacht, and what all does the policy cover?

Does the yacht have GPS on board, or do you have to bring your own handheld unit as well as a sextant, tables, and chronometer?

Are there charts on board to cover the entire route home?

Does the owner insist on a full crew that you have to supply, or is it OK for you to single-hand it?

Will your one-way airfare be paid by the owner, or is it included in the fee you charge?

Is there a time limit put on your return date? This can present a real problem if you are depending on sail power. You never know what Neptune might hand you in the way of wind direction and strength.

Crossing an ocean, especially beating hard on the wind for long periods, can be hard on any yacht, as well as the crew; how much cleanup will you be expected to do when the boat is back in her berth?

The payment schedule should be worked out to protect both the owner and the delivery captain. The going rate in 1998, according to one delivery skipper, was $2.50 per mile sailed. Of course this is always negotiable, depending on whether the delivery is expected to be mostly downwind and relatively easy, or a more difficult upwind trip.

A friend of mine when in Tahiti during a long cruise across the Pacific, left his boat securely anchored in a bay in Moorea, with a Tahitian to keep an eye on it. He then delivered a yacht back to California. He claimed that the fee he received for the delivery would keep him cruising for almost a year.

When you board an owner's yacht, it is up to you to really check out and verify that everything important really does work properly. If you find something unsafe, which might put your life in jeopardy, the problem must be repaired or replaced before you put to sea, or you may decide the boat is not really seaworthy and turn down the delivery. You are the one to make the decision. Your life and the lives of your crew may depend on your judgment.

If there is no time limit to get the boat home to its berth, you may have an enjoyable cruise back, being able to stop at islands on your route. Breaking up the trip into two or three legs gives your crew a much-needed rest at times.

Once you make a name for yourself as being dependable, you can build up your business. I know a delivery captain who works almost continuously, making a very good living. He appears to really enjoy a healthy life, being out in the fresh ocean air most of the time.

CREW ON LARGE LUXURY YACHTS

There are always openings for crew needed on large yachts, some of which rarely leave the home base, being used for entertaining more than anything else. I knew an owner with a 60-foot motor yacht who entertained friends almost every weekend, yet the yacht left the berth only a couple of times a year, one of these times being to haul her out for bottom painting. Of course, this kind of yacht needs only a chef, someone to serve drinks and food, and a clean-up crew.

If a large yacht is used a lot, it is necessary for the owner to either work like a slave keeping up with regular maintenance and cleaning, or be forced to hire a crew. Even if the boat is seldom moved, it takes many hours to keep the boat clean. There are lots of different systems to maintain on a large yacht, so there may be a place for your talents. There is a different kind of feeling when you work on a boat rather than at some job that you absolutely hate. Even if the money is less for working on a boat, it is often worth it to be away from a stressful city job.

I have met up with large yachts cruising to distant ports, and most have extensive crew. One such motor yacht, actually more like a ship, being 180 feet long, had a crew of seven. They were told by the owner to take the yacht to a particular port, be there on a certain date, and the owners would join them for only a few days.

It was then decided where the crew would take the yacht next, and off they would go again, and so the yacht was working its way around the world, visiting all the most exotic places. The crewmembers had a marvelous time, with little pressure on them until the owners arrived, which was only occasionally.

Of course, there are also people who crewed on yachts and had not so pleasant an experience. I have heard stories of captains who made Captain Bligh look like a nice, pleasant, helpful, kind soul in comparison. Owners also have been described as miserable slavedrivers, expecting the crew to be on duty at all times, with no time off to call their own.

So it is important to look for a position on a yacht that appears to be a happy, well-run boat, with reasonable owners and an experienced, fair captain.

We were anchored in the Marquesas when a small ketch sailed into the bay. Within minutes of setting the anchor, a man and two women climbed into their dinghy and rowed for shore. However, when the dinghy had just touched the beach, the two women jumped out onto the sand as the man threw their bags out onto the beach and quickly rowed back to the ketch.

We later learned from the women that they had joined the ketch in California six weeks earlier and had had a nightmare trip with a skipper/owner who was demented. During their crossing he either did not know where they were on the ocean, or just would not tell them. They sailed on day after day, not knowing when they would arrive anywhere. The skipper had expected them to do more than crew duties; when they wouldn't accept his advances, he became very angry and acted crazy.

It is important for you to interview the owners--or captain, if he is the person hiring the crew--while he is interviewing you. Satisfy yourself that the job suits you. It is not always easy to jump ship, especially if you are already committed to an ocean crossing.

It is more usual that the crew is happy to be partaking in a trip that they normally wouldn't have the opportunity to make, but the unhappy crew members do much more talking about bad experiences.

CRUISING PHYSICIAN

Cruising sailors are often far from a doctor, and there are always things cropping up that would make a doctor very welcome. (Of course, to make money this way you must be a genuine physician.) Even doctors need cruising cash, and there is always a need for one, especially in the outer islands, where doctors visit very occasionally.

If you are a doctor and are cruising, hang out your physician's pennant and you may be swamped with people needing your skills. Even if the natives cannot pay in cash, you will not want for fish, fruit, vegetables, or other trading goods. It has been my experience that

most islanders are very generous with whatever they have.

On the island of Huahine, a fairly primitive place in French Polynesia, as we walked along the crushed coral road we were invited into the home of a Polynesian family. The family obviously had very little in the way of material wealth, but after offering us fruit, bananas, papaya, pineapple, what came out next but an almost-full bottle of Chevas Regal brandy. This must have been a real treasure of theirs, but they were anxious to share it with us. I felt guilty not having anything with us to offer them, so we invited them to come for dinner on the yacht and they really enjoyed the evening on the American boat.

I had an interesting visit with a French doctor in Rangiroa, in the Tuamotus Islands. I had been riding our fold-up bicycle to the post office and stopped to look around a small graveyard by a church. Later, as we were having dinner on *Seahorse*, I asked the doctor why the local graveyard had so many headstones for young children, eight, nine, ten, eleven, and twelve years old. I was astounded to hear him say that most died from dehydration. He claimed there was a fine line between thirst and the point of dehydration when the person will not drink.

The children perspire with the tropic heat, and the parents bundle them up in case they get a cold; pretty soon the kids are in real trouble. If they are not taken to a doctor, the end is close for them. The doctor said it was miraculous to see the change in a child, almost at the point of death, coming right back to health immediately he got fluid into them.

I had a problem with a crewmember crossing the ocean. After fifteen days at sea, and being over seasickness, a crewman told me that Brad had not eaten or drunk anything for a couple of days. I could hardly believe it, but immediately got out the salt tablets and a bottle of water. It took a lot of persuasion to get Brad to take either the salt tablets or the water. I had to threaten to pour the water down his throat. He kept maintaining that he was OK. However, after he drank a glass of water, suddenly he wanted more and more, and then he was hungry, really hungry. I don't know how many glasses of water Brad downed, but he became normal very quickly. I had not even thought about dehydration being a problem. All the seasickness had been finished with a few days after leaving California. I guess it can start at any time, if a person perspires too much and forgets to drink something.

If you are a doctor and are cruising to distant ports, let people know of your skills. You will be in demand wherever you travel.

DENTIST ON DUTY

I met Dr. Simpson when he was building a 50-foot steel ketch. His plan was to eventually give up his practice of dentistry and head for the South Seas, possibly going all around the world. He planned a large aftercabin to be his office, with a full-size dentist's chair, including all the necessary tools and equipment, drills, polishers, et cetera. Dr. Simpson was planning to keep his cruising kitty going by working at teeth wherever he went. Again, there are always people needing dental repairs, but they may be miles and miles from a dentist on duty.

The Polynesians have notoriously poor teeth. I met a dentist in Tahiti; he was attending a dental conference to discuss the Polynesian problem, but when I talked to him they had not yet hit on the trouble. The dentist thought it was their diet. The fact is that it would almost be a full-time job for a dentist anywhere he would cruise in Polynesia.

Polynesians are not the only ones in need of dentistry. There are numerous sailors and their families making their way around the world. Sometimes teeth get damaged, etc., and it would be wonderful if a dentist were available.

BARBER ON DUTY

It is not very difficult to set your boat up as a traveling barbershop. One cabin can suffice, and you don't need a swivel, hydraulic barber chair, though I'm sure this would make things more comfortable for the barber, being able to raise and lower the person in the chair. I am sure that there are barbers the world over who do not have great hydraulic barber chairs, yet still do a good job at hair cutting. (When I was a boy, growing up in Ireland, the barber had a regular chair but used a larger cushion, or even a board across the arm rests, for little kids to sit up on.)

Wherever you go there are people who get their hair cut, so if you are skilled at hair cutting, put up a sign. Let the locals know. You can have a strip of sailcloth made up like a striped barber pole, and fly it from the rigging--also a flag showing "barber on duty."

If you are going to wash and rinse every customer's hair, you may need reasonably large water tanks or may have to install a water maker on board. Of course this will not be necessary if you are berthed in a marina with water and electricity hookups.

Men's hair is usually fairly simple to cut, though nowadays even men have some fancy hairstyles. Maybe you are a skilled hair stylist able to accommodate both men and women. This is all the more reason to set up shop from your boat.

While you are living on your boat your expenses are minimal, and any money made, prolongs your cruising schedule and keeps you away from the rat race (or civilization, as we call it).

CARPENTER FOR HIRE

When you are cruising you spend a lot of time in different harbors, many of them berthing boats owned by people too busy to take care of their crafts. If the word gets around that you are a skilled woodworker, you may find all kinds of opportunities to make money altering some cabinetry or making changes in seating or closets. You can line a clothes locker with cedar or make more drawers and fit them into a blank space. There are never enough drawers in a boat.

You may have to put up a sign or notice in the harbor office explaining your skills. Even the harbormaster may need your services repairing docks or walkways around the marina where you are berthed. The harbormaster might know which owner would most likely need your services. Marinas often have a bulletin board on which you can post your card or message.

If you have built your own yacht, you are skilled in many ways. These skills are useful to local boatyards, most of which are constantly looking for skilled craftsmen. Visit around the different yards. You may only want to work part time; this also suits some businesses who will hire help when they get busy.

Even a large boatyard can get busy in a hurry if they get in a boat that was burned or partially submerged. Either of these situations creates a lot of work for a lot of employees.

If you are in an area where boats are being built, there may be openings for your services. You may not know of a boat builder near your berth, but check it out. Many boats are built a long way from the water, lifted onto trucks when finished, and trucked to a launching place by the water.

The marine field is a very large industry presenting lots of opportunities for anyone who wants work.

Maintain and Repair Boats   24

Painting Contracting

Around the yacht harbor there is always paint work needing to be done. Put out the word that you are available for repainting and refinishing. Most people have had experience painting during their lifetimes--fences, gates, doors, rooms, and so forth--and refinishing boats is not very different.

Most fiberglass boats are finished in gel coat, an epoxy resin with color that lasts for years. The modern finishes like Awlgrip and Sterling, to mention just two, are extremely hard-wearing and last as long as gel coat. Despite this there are many yachts finished with regular paints, even house paints, that need refinishing regularly.

Most marinas and yacht harbors prohibit any type of spray painting, so you are limited to doing it by hand, which, with a little practice, can still produce a fine finish as long as you use good brushes and paint made or thinned with a retarder for brushing.

Get business cards printed--they don't cost much--offering your services refinishing yacht interiors, exteriors, and so on. Leave one on each boat in the harbor. You might distribute them around the neighborhood and offer to do house painting also.

If you are not very experienced, you may enlist the help of your local paint store. They will explain in detail each step in the whole process of painting. They will explain each material you will require, and how to prepare the surface. Then you will be all set.

VARNISHING

There is a never-ending job on boats with brightwork, or woodwork that has been beautifully built with expensive lumber, then finished with varnish. There is almost nothing more beautiful than a yacht with all the brightwork gleaming, smooth as silk, with the wood grain showing through the transparent finish.

In the tropics, or where the sun shines almost every day, varnish needs to be redone almost every three months. Of course, many owners have covers they button on for the times the boat is not used; however, though covers help a lot, pretty soon the woodwork must be revarnished.

It would seem to a neophyte that varnishing is a very difficult occupation, but actually it's not, if you have the patience to sand all the varnish work with a fine grit sandpaper until the finish is smooth. Wash the whole thing down with fresh water and a sponge, dry it off completely, and you are almost ready to brush on the varnish. Tape with masking tape everything you might accidentally brush or drip onto, and cover teak or painted decks with masking paper or plastic; now you are ready to use the brush.

One of the most important tools of the refinisher is the brush. This must be the finest you can buy, and when you pay a lot of money for a brush you must take proper care of it. Clean it completely immediately you are finished applying coats.

One step I neglected to mention is the necessity of a vacuum cleaner to remove every speck of dust that might be in your area after you have sanded. Dust is the nightmare of varnish refinishers, and all sanded surfaces must be wiped over with a tack rag before varnish is applied. There is also the problem of the wind starting to blow just as you have started to varnish. Blowing dust can make a mess. All the work must be done again from scratch. Few will take the chance to varnish on a windy day.

There is a lot of varnish work to be done in every marina and yacht harbor, and people who do this type of work in the fresh air would find it very hard to go back to being indoors all day. They work mostly in the outdoors, without a boss breathing down their necks. There is also great satisfaction admiring the completed job.

BOAT CLEANING AND WAXING

Maybe you do not want to do anything too technical or mind-taxing. There is always work around boat marinas or harbors keeping yachts shipshape and in Bristol fashion. Many owners would rather pay another to wash and clean their boat, sometimes once a month or more frequently.

One enterprising young man I know in Sausalito, California has quite a good little business going with three and four employees doing a lot of the work. They service yachts, washing and waxing, cleaning interiors, checking and filling water tanks, and other service work; some of these yachts they clean once a week whether they have been used or not.

You might find a hobby job turning into a real business. At times I have been asked if I knew anyone dependable to keep a boat clean, so there is a market for this kind of service.

Waxing is another service, though it is a little more work waxing a boat than washing one. However, the job pays a lot more money and the finished product is more beautiful and a pleasure to look upon. Yacht finishes gradually deteriorate in the marine atmosphere, the sun doing even more damage than the salt water. Before waxing a boat that has faded with the weather, it may be necessary to buff the finish first with a cleaner to bring back the shiny finish, then wax it to keep it that way.

There are many different waxes on the market, some easier to apply than others. Usually the types more difficult to apply seem to last longer, or maybe this is only imagined because of the extra labor expended. Even applying the wipe-on-and-wipe-off wax cleaners helps the look of a boat a great deal.

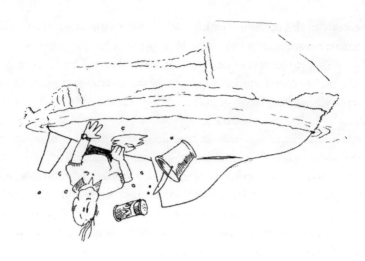

BOTTOM CLEANING/ZINC CHANGING

Harbors berth many boats whose owners are concerned about keeping their boats in top condition. There is a big market for bottom cleaning. Keeping algae and other marine organisms from growing and developing on the boat bottom is a continual nuisance for boat owners. From the smallest boat to the largest ship, if she is kept in salt water, even brackish water, stuff grows on the bottom from the waterline down to the bottom of the keel.

Painting boat hulls from the waterline down with anti-fouling paint stops the growth of marine organisms as long as the paint has not worn off. Bottom paint is generally soft and actually chalks off as time goes by, until most of the toxicity has worn away. Barnacles and weeds start to grow fairly quickly, fouling the hull, causing loss of speed.

If the boat is not hauled and cleaned for a long period of time, the propeller will be so fouled with barnacles that the propellor blades resemble round balls and the motor will not be able to move the hull through the water.

Owners who race their boat and need every bit of speed they can get, will either haul out and clean the bottom before each race, or dive underwater and scrub the bottom. However, hauling before every race can be very expensive, and many people do not like diving in cold water.

This is the reason there are opportunities for a person with a wetsuit, mask and snorkel, flippers, and some scrubbing gear to make money scrubbing boat bottoms. Many bottom cleaners use some kind of scuba or compressor on the dock to supply air while they scrub continuously, also a suction cup or plumber's helper to hold themselves close to the hull.

It is necessary to scrub the scum and whiskers off the bottom if you are going to race, but without scrubbing, the paint will last longer, doing a good job for more than a year, even longer, if the water is cold like the northern California coast water. The sooner the paint is scrubbed off, the sooner the barnacles can start to grow.

A much more important task for the diver is to check and change the zincs which are eaten away. When different metals are immersed in salt water, electrolysis will cause the less noble metal to dissipate into the water, causing serious damage to valves, propellers, bearings, through-hull fittings, or any metal that is under water. To protect these metals, adequate blocks of zinc are fastened to the hull, preferably near the metal parts. Zincs are less noble than any other metal on a boat, so they are sacrificial anodes. Electrolysis works on the zincs as long as they are there, and when all the zinc blocks are gone, the next noble metal will start to suffer.

Divers normally check the zincs when they are under water; it is usually a fairly easy job to change them. Zincs are extremely important, since a hull with electrolysis problems can cost a fortune to repair if it is allowed to stay in salt water with no zinc protection.

REPAIRING FIBERGLASS

The majority of boats in marinas and yacht harbors are manufactured of fiberglass materials. Sooner or later they get dinged up, hitting the dock or another boat. They sometimes crack from weather or fatigue, and need repairs.

Many fiberglass problems can be taken care of using only a small hand grinder to remove damaged or cracked material. This allows you to lay in glass cloth and epoxy resin until the necessary buildup of material is accomplished. Sanding will smooth the finish ready for painting, or for the right color of gel-coat to be applied.

I do not want to sound as if this work is really simple; it takes practice and skill. Even the mixing of the epoxies must be followed carefully, according to the manufacturer's specifications. Also, certain materials will not adhere well to other materials. If you are in doubt, call the material manufacturers or the suppliers for the proper instructions. They will be glad to assist you.

Probably the worst thing about fiberglass repairing is the dust created by sanding or grinding this material. Using a strong vacuum cleaner attached to the sander will help. If you are not completely covered by protective clothing from head to foot, using paper suits, head socks, eye shields, a good respirator, and gloves with arm sleeves taped over the gloves, you may still get glass dust on your skin. This can create the most uncomfortable itch, which even vigorous showering does not always cure.

There is a lot of fiberglass work around, and not enough guys to do it--at least, this has been my observation in northern California. Though it is dusty work, it pays fairly well. I have even known a few men who enjoyed repairing or even building things out of fiberglass.

It really is a wonderful material for boat construction, as long as it is properly laid up, without voids or flaws that might create blisters in the future.

GLASS WORK

Perhaps you are skilled at changing window glass, or removing and replacing window frames. Some of the greatest headaches that plague boat owners are caused by leaking windows--sliding glass windows, especially. Even fixed ports give problems. Caulking dries out, cracks, and shrinks.

And it is possible they were never sealed correctly from the factory. One large corporation that I know of manufactures many yachts every year. They use the best of equipment and accessories, but unfortunately they are careless about the bedding of these to the hull; this carelessness causes frequent leaks.

To establish exactly where the leak is, have someone inside the boat watch the area where the water enters the boat while you spray the exterior with a water hose, starting at a lower area for a while, then spraying farther up. If it doesn't leak into the inside, raise the spray to a higher area and continue to spray specific areas until the assistant inside yells that the water has started to seep in.

When you have located the area of the leak, check every fitting on the outside. Everything that is fitted must have a bedding of caulk underneath it. It may be necessary to remove fittings to rebed them before refastening them to the hull. This goes for all screw holes or anything that enters the hull.

Window channels must have drain holes to the outside, allowing the water to drain away before the water rises to the level of the inner edge of the channel and flows into the boat. These drain holes or scupper slots in the outside rail often get plugged with dirt and debris. These drain holes must be completely cleared. Often just clearing these drain holes or slots will rectify a serious leaking problem.

It may be necessary to remove the complete frame, including the glass. Then dismantle the entire unit, if the problem is with the frame. Reassembling with the proper caulking or bedding compound will usually cure the problem.

Hatches, especially sliding hatches, are a frequent source of leak problems on many boats. Sometimes the original design is faulty, and little can be done to cure the problems without major redesigning and/or reconstructing the hatch properly. Usually, however, a study of the leak problem and a little common sense will give a solution as to how to cure the leak.

I am sure with a little advertising of the fact that you trace and fix leaks in windows, hatches and hulls, there would be a lot of demand for your services around the marinas. Leak detecting and repairing is not usually a very demanding job mentally, but it takes a lot of time and patience, which, if you live on your boat or are cruising, you have in abundance.

RIGGING AND SAIL REPAIRS

In every yacht harbor there are sailboats that sooner or later need to have the rigging—the wires that hold up the mast—replaced because of stretching or fracturing ends. Quite a few years ago, most rigging was made out of steel cable galvanized to keep it from rusting, but eventually it rusted anyway. With the advent of stainless steel, it was thought that the rigging would last forever. However, most rigging experts claim that even stainless steel wire deteriorates as tiny cracks form in swaging where the ends are fastened to the wire, making it necessary to replace most standing rigging after ten years of use.

The running rigging used to haul up sails and so forth is not so critical, since a failure of a halyard only lets a sail fall down to the deck. This is nothing like the disaster caused by a failure in the standing rigging that lets the mast fall down, which can destroy or sink the boat. When the mast goes over the side, the rigging wires stay attached, and the mast and spreaders may damage or puncture the hull—or worse, maim or kill a crew person.

There is always work for a person skilled in rigging repairs. This may be only splicing eyes in the end of dock lines, or it may be more involved jobs up the mast, requiring hauling yourself up on a bosun's chair—or seat, as it actually is.

If you have to completely replace all the standing rigging on a boat, the mast has to be unstepped, which will allow you to remove all the wires. You can then send everything to a rigging shop. They will make all new wiring, the exact same size and length as the old ones. Then it is a simple task to put everything back the same as before, and the boat is now completely rerigged. Turnbuckles should also be replaced at this time, or they and the rigging can be sent to have everything x-rayed, which shows up any flaw in the stainless steel.

Servicing winches is a necessary time consumer that must be carried out every so often. When the winch feels stiff or difficult to turn, or the little stopper teeth stick, not holding the winch from turning backwards, then you know it is time to disassemble, clean, and regrease all the parts, and reassemble the winch again.

Winches are generally simple to take apart and just as simple to reassemble, though care should be taken not to allow the coil retaining spring to fly out of your hands and go overboard. A few spare retainer springs should always be carried on board. Winch handles also need a little lubrication of the lock-in mechanism; otherwise, the handle becomes difficult to lock in or remove from the winch. A little WD40 sprayed on them occasionally usually takes care of the winch handles.

Turning blocks—in fact, all rigging blocks—need to be flushed occasionally with fresh water, to remove salt deposits. Salt makes them difficult to turn, and adds much friction to their operation. After drying, the blocks may be sprayed with WD40, which makes them run even smoother.

It is necessary to have a heavy-duty sewing machine operating on electricity if you are going to do sail repairs, though many of the reinforcing corner patches and work around cringles, etc., are done by hand sewing. There are a number of small sewing machines on the market, like the Read's Sailmaker machine manufactured in England, which will sew through three to five layers of sail dacron. For a small machine, they will do quite a lot of heavy work.

There is always a demand for splicing lines. Making loops in the ends of dock lines makes it much simpler to dock or berth the boat. Splicing ropes or even wire cable can make quite a lot of money, because it takes a lot of time.

CLEAN AND FILTER FUEL TANKS

When diesel fuel sits for a long time in a tank, it can develop problems; a type of algae will grow in the fuel, and this in turn will quickly clog up filters and fuel lines. There are different additives that can be put into the tank when taking on fuel, which greatly inhibit the growth of these algae. Otherwise it is necessary to recirculate the fuel through filters for quite a while until the fuel is clean. This is called fuel polishing.

Various companies perform this service. It can be performed either from a truck or from a boat coming alongside the boat needing the fuel cleaned. The service person removes an inspection plate in the top of the fuel tank, inserts into the bottom of the tank a suction hose from a large-capacity suction pump in the service truck or boat, and pumps the fuel through a number of filters back into the tank. The pump circulates the fuel quickly and continuously, until the filters pick up most of the dirt in the tank.

If the tank does not have an inspection plate, a fuel hose must be disconnected, or a drain plug tapped into, if there is a valve on the drain. The fuel polishing service person usually wants the tank to be at least 60 percent full.

There is money to be made cleaning diesel tanks, since there are only a few companies doing this service. In the greater San Francisco Bay area, there are only two or three that I know of. With the proper pump and filters it is not a difficult job.

SERVICE AND PUMP OUT HOLDING TANKS

Toilets in boats must have holding tanks or a very capable purification system before waste can be pumped into the sea or a bay. This necessitates going to a pump-out station every so often, to have the waste tank emptied.

There are companies who do this service for your boat on a weekly or longer time basis, or on call, depending on how much you use your boat, your boat's tank's capacity, and so forth. They will come by boat, connect their suction hose to your waste discharge fitting on deck, start pumping, and in a very short time, voilá, your tank is empty. This service can be performed using a fairly small 18- to 25-foot boat, though it has to have a large holding tank installed, since some of the yachts serviced have two, three, or more holding tanks.

This service is not expensive, and having it done on a regular basis saves an owner the bother of continually running over to the pump-out station, which may or may not be open. Even when you go there, they may have a number of boats ahead of yours waiting their turn.

Though this may be a slightly odorous occupation, there is a market for this service. Especially as our society becomes more affluent, more and larger yachts appear, and boating becomes the only way to get away from the usual crowds. They all have to have waste holding tanks, and they all get filled up, no matter how you try to avoid it.

If you are mechanically minded and have skilled hands, there is always lots of work to be done around a marina or yacht harbor. Boats—especially large yachts—have many complicated systems, and most mechanical things require regular servicing and maintenance.

If there is a bulletin or message board in the marina office, put up your ad explaining your capabilities, the systems you service, engines, transmissions, fuel systems, cooling systems, et cetera. If you specialize in particular engine types, diesel or gasoline, makes or models, mention this also. Many owners feel better having their particular engine worked on by someone who specializes in their particular model.

If there is a boat yard in your area, check with them in case they are busy and need extra help.

Leave your card on all the larger yachts, especially if they appear to be well kept up. Usually if the boat looks as though no one ever goes near it, probably the owner is not interested in spending money on it. Appearance is a good indication of how the owner feels about his boat.

A concerned owner may be interested in having you run his engine/engines once every week, also checking and running generators and making sure the batteries are charged up and all systems ready to go any time the owner wishes to use his yacht. There is always work for a good mechanic.

SERVICE OUTBOARD MOTORS

Outboard motors are not, as a rule, extremely complicated machines. Usually servicing them is limited to changing the spark plugs; greasing the zerk fittings, so that everything moves freely; and maybe checking and adjusting the timing of the spark.

If the motor has not been run in a long time, the gasoline may be old and may have lost its potency. The gas needs to be replaced with new gasoline.

Also the carburetor may be gummed up with dried-up oil and gasoline mix. This usually necessitates removing and disassembling the carburetor, cleaning everything—the bowl, the jets, and washing and blowing out the tiny airways—reassembling the carburetor, checking the float, and installing the carburetor on the motor. When everything is clean, checked, and there is a good spark at the plugs, the motor should run.

Lots of owners do not bother doing normal service on their outboard motors, so there is a market for servicing them. You may also be aligned with a motor distributor, and may sell outboard motors from your boat. Small outboards are easily handled, though now some models with two hundred horsepower and more weigh so much that you need a crane or lifting device to pick them up and move them around. But these large motors are the exception rather than the rule. Marinas are full of boats with small outboard motors, lots of them needing service of one kind or another.

There may even be service work needed to repair dinghies and small yacht tenders; this can be done on the dock. One often sees an inflatable dinghy partly deflated lying in the water, showing that no one has bothered with it in some time. The owner might be glad to have you service it and get it shipshape again.

REPAIRING ELECTRICAL SYSTEMS

One of the most difficult systems to keep working perfectly in the marine environment is the electrical system. Salt-laden air plays havoc with electrical connections, causing corrosion and bad continuity of electrical current, especially low voltage current. Most boats have 12-volt systems that need to be kept clean and dry. If a boat is left unattended for long periods of time, it is good to leave a low power heater switched on, to keep the interior dry.

If you are skilled in electrical system repairs, hang up your shingle. You may be swamped with requests for your services. Boat yards in Northern California charge up to $90.00 per hour for a skilled craftsman to work on a boat, creating a situation where freelance craftsmen offer their services for much less than boat yards charge. Even boat yard employees often do moonlight jobs, nights or weekends.

The market is there, especially in a larger marina where there are lots of yachts berthed. You might be called for some insignificant little job that doesn't seem worth bothering with, but another time it could possibly lead to rebuilding a complete system. A boat that has had a fire on board or that has been a partial sinker needs extensive rebuilding.

There's lots of this type of work everywhere boats are kept.

METAL WORK AND WELDING

Cruising boats usually have a fair-sized engine, making it possible to add a generator large enough to power a welding machine. On our cruise in 1973, we had a 5-kw generator set in the engine room. Though this powers just about the smallest arc welding machine, we were able to help other cruisers who had broken gear, stainless steel fittings that had come apart, and other problems. We were happy to repair these things, and though we didn't charge for the services, we usually were repaid in other ways, with gifts of food, and so forth. We had not advertised the fact that we did welding, though I think that if we had done so, there would have been a demand for our services.

Of course, if you are planning to cruise and make money repairing metal problems, you have to have a selection of different types of welding rods, to cover welding steel or stainless steel. You need brazing rods for brass or bronze or copper. Other tools and equipment will be necessary additions to your tool room.

If you are going to do extensive metal work, you will need an oxygen/acetylene cutting and welding set. If space is limited, small cylinders are available; these last quite a while and do a lot of work.

A hand grinder is also a must. This has many uses and is handy for all kinds of jobs.

You will need drilling and tapping tools, and all the usual fix-it hand tools. This equipment will also be useful for making objects of art, if you lean towards creating things.

All kinds of metal scrap can be obtained from a local junk or scrap yard. Your imagination will dictate what you can make from what you have on hand. A look around some novelty stores will show you all kinds of objects to be made out of nuts, bolts, washers, and the like. Some eye-catching sculptures have been created by persons who have only the most rudimentary metalworking or welding skills.

MAKING MONEY WITH YOUR BOAT

Electronics Sales and Service

There was a time when boats and yachts were simple, uncomplicated things, the purists not wanting anything more than a hull and sails, or on a powerboat, the simplest means of propulsion. Nowadays, however, the purist ideals have diminished, and boats have become completely self sufficient, with every type of gear and convenience imaginable.

It was once claimed that the marine environment was too harsh for any electrical systems to survive, but now, even small boats have all kinds of electrical and electronic equipment on board. Electrical and electronic systems do suffer in the salt-water environment, but keeping them clean and dry and using them regularly will extend their life indefinitely.

If you possess skills in electronics operation and repair, there is lots of work in this field. Even compass adjusting and compensating is a field with very few individuals competing for the business, possibly because not many people are trained or skilled in this occupation.

There is a system now, where the compass is removed from the boat, to an area where there is no large amount of metal that will influence the compass. There the compass is adjusted, using an instrument to remove all deviation. Then the instrument is put back into the boat and again adjusted to remove any remaining errors caused by the boat's magnetic interference.

Compass compensating is a skill not known by many people. When I was getting the compass on my steel ketch *Seahorse 2* before setting off for the South Seas, the technician told me that the last job he had to do was the main compass on the U. S. Navy aircraft carrier *Coral Sea*. Apparently the Navy had had such an error in *Coral Sea*'s compass for so many years that they had considered rebuilding the whole bridge area out of aluminum. The technician told me that he was able to remove almost all the errors in the compass. He also enjoyed the heady feeling when he was commanding the ship as to what course to steer next, for the great ship would swing around to answer his commands. He was also very proud of the cap they had given him, with all the scrambled egg on it and the *Coral Sea* name embroidered on it.

There is work to do in the field of electronics if you have or can acquire the skills to do it. The more you get into it, the more equipment like radars and radios you may be able to supply, making a profit on the equipment as well as the installation labor.

PLUMBING & REFRIGERATION SERVICING

Marine plumbing systems are simpler than those found in home construction, if only for the simple reason that most of the piping can be traced inside lockers or cupboards, under flooring hatches, or behind removable panels. Boats also may have a plumbing diagram supplied by the manufacturer, and this greatly assists in repairing problems in the piping system.

Of course some manufacturers bury some parts in the fiberglass, but generally hoses and wiring are installed after the hull is finished, making repairs more easily accomplished. Water systems in boats are often plumbed with flexible plastic hose secured with hose clamps; this type of installation can be easily changed without soldering, as would be needed with hard copper piping.

At one time boats were fairly simple, without complicated electrical or electronics systems, but now air conditioners, heating systems, water makers, and many other amenities are common place. The marine environment creates quite a lot of work for service technicians to keep complicated systems working smoothly.

Air conditioning and refrigeration systems are a specialized field, but if you have experience working with them, there is a market for your expertise. One plus is the fact that a refrigeration service technician does not need a zillion dollars' worth of tools, or specialized equipment, to accomplish the work. Usually the necessary equipment can be taken to the boat in a couple of small toolboxes; also a vacuum pump may be needed, which is transportable on a regular hand truck.

Of course there may be times when other pieces of equipment

are in the way of servicing the refrigeration system. This obstructing equipment has to be removed, to facilitate working on the unit needing service. The complete air-conditioner or refrigeration unit may have to be removed from the boat, which can be a heavy job, depending on the size of the units. It might require two or more men to lift them.

Because so many boats, especially larger yachts, have air-conditioners, refrigerators, and freezers, there is lots of work to do in this field.

HYDRAULIC SERVICE AND REPAIRS

Hydraulics, from anchor windlasses to power roller furling systems, have become more and more used in yachts, especially in mega yachts. Hydraulic power is used to drive bow thrusters, stern thrusters, automatic stabilizers, and a host of other things. Probably the biggest users of hydraulic power are fishing boats, particularly heavy drag boats, with giant hoisting winches, booms and slings, and so forth. Hydraulic systems, when they are designed correctly and set up properly, work tirelessly for years without problems, except for the need for servicing and changing filters, fluid, and occasionally a worn hydraulic hose.

It is not necessary for a hydraulics service person to have a lot of expensive equipment. Hydraulic supply companies will give a person all kinds of directions as to what you need to repair a system. They will make up any size hose to the exact length you order, with the proper fittings swaged onto the ends. Then it is only a matter of your removing an old hose and pulling in the new one.

Once you understand the principles of hydraulics, it is fairly simple to effect repairs, though it is sometimes heavy work. The larger hoses are extremely stiff, heavy, and hard to work into an awkward place.

If you are a pretty good mechanic, get a book on hydraulics; you will be amazed at how easily you get used to it and how much money you might make. Before you know it, you could be redesigning complete systems.

One of the most important things about working on hydraulic systems, is the need for everything to be spotlessly clean. The system must be well filtered, even when every single component is air-blown clean before assembly. This includes new hoses; after they have been made, it is extremely important that every speck of dust be blown out of them with a high-pressure airline.

When disassembling hydraulic systems or replacing multiple hoses, it is a good idea to cap or plug the ends, both to stop fluid leaking everywhere and to keep the system clean. Caps and plugs can be matched, with numbers stamped into them, a cap and a plug having the same number. This will make it easy to reinstall the hoses to the proper line, the same as they were before. Having the hoses identified makes it possible to remove numerous hoses at the same time, get new hoses made up, change over the caps or plugs and reinstall them easily, without mixing up the hydraulic flow or screwing up the system.

The more you get into hydraulics, the more you will enjoy the fantastic power they can create. With a single little lever, you have tremendous power at your fingertips.

SELL YOUR CREATIVITY 25

PHOTOGRAPHY

There are numerous photographers who make a very nice livelihood taking pictures. With a reasonably good camera, a bit of training, and a lot of patience, you could possibly add a lot to your income.

Who can dispute the beautiful scenery around boats and water, with the ever-changing hues and vistas? Life studies of sea birds, seagulls, sandpipers, terns, kingfishers, egrets, and in California the great blue heron, all make marvelous pictures. An unusual sunset or sunrise, a special scene, or an area that might interest tourists, could be the basis for a set of postcards, always in demand. Even an old derelict boat, hauled up on the beach to die, can be an eye-catching subject. Everywhere you look, an old seaport will reveal wonderful true-to-life interests.

Photographed from the water, sailboats gliding along gracefully or fighting to get ahead in a race can make pictures of great interest, especially to the particular owner of the boat that you photographed. If you have the use of a high-speed boat, you can scoot around getting pictures of yachts, both power and sail—even great megayachts. This type of photography is always in vogue. The ever-popular boating scene presents many interesting photographic subjects, including beautiful sunbronzed, swimsuited girls with the wind in their hair.

Cameras are so improved nowadays, that some fantastic photographs are possible using the simplest modern camera, though I am sure that a professional photographer will maintain that it is necessary to have really expensive equipment. I'm sure this may be the case. It is generally a fact that the better the tools, the better the workmanship. I have seen beautiful work done by men with a simple, inadequate tool kit, but it takes an excellent craftsman to accomplish a beautifully finished product with inferior equipment.

The latest digital cameras simplify picture taking, for their photos can be immediately viewed, changed, erased, and taken over, until you have exactly the results you desire. There is the possibility of taking video movies and making a photograph from any of the still shots in the video. Videotapes can be used over and over again, without the great cost of taking movie film, including the added expense of developing.

MAKING AND SELLING PAINTINGS AND SCULPTURES

If you have a little drawing talent and have lots of time on your hands (which is usual when you live on your boat), take a few lessons and start drawing and painting. The scenery around boats and docks lends itself very easily to the artist. Water scenes are always changing color, and changing from calm, like a sheet of glass, creating reflections wonderful to capture on canvas, to wind-whipped whitecaps sweeping across the surface, with spindrift blowing away in the wind. As a student in school, I was always happy drawing seascapes. They seemed to be easier to draw than other types of scenery.

It always amazes me how talented many people are when they take the time to try something new. Often after a person retires, they start a whole new career, sometimes being more successful with the "hobby" than they were in the business or profession at which they had spent their entire working life.

Painting and sculpting are fun to learn, and there are always classes being given in the local colleges. Then it is just a matter of your spending the time putting down on canvas what you see around you. Put the painting in a nice frame, and you have a saleable item.

Having your boat allows you to move easily to different locations where you can see a glorious sunset or sunrise through the rigging of another boat. Some artists I have known take a photograph of a beautiful scene, then recreate the photo on a canvas. No matter how you do it, you will have fun. You will satisfy your creative instincts, and you may even make money doing something you really enjoy.

Sculpting is another pastime that some people have a real talent for. This also takes time and if you live the simple life on your boat, you do have time to give to a hobby like this, which will also bring in some cash when you sell your sculptures.

There is a lot of satisfaction in creating a figure or scene out of clay or plaster, and who knows, you may have another Leonardo da Vinci hidden inside you, or Picasso, and that couldn't be all that difficult.

Your boat makes it possible to be in places that can only be seen from the water. This gives you the advantage of capturing beautiful scenes that many other people cannot visit.

Boat Lettering and Signs

There are always boat owners wanting name changes, retouching the lettering on their boat, or fancy script work done. You may be talented at this skill, or you may be a good craftsman, capable of laying out signs and lettering.

Nowadays some of the best sign painters do much of the layup work on computers. They also make stencils that greatly assist them in making a beautiful sign. The stencil is often made with paper or plastic sheet having an adhesive on one side covered by a peel-off paper. When the stencil is completely cut out, the backing is pulled off and the stencil is adhered to the boat. The necessary parts are then peeled off, allowing the craftsman to spray or paint in the lettering or striping.

There are also plastic letters similar to the above, but these letters themselves stick right on the yacht after you peel off the backing material. These systems of lettering are becoming more and more popular.

Sign painting with brush and paint is much more difficult. This also requires the proper paintbrushes, which make it possible to paint in detail with a fine line. A cheap throw-away brush just will not do it.

With the right equipment and some practice you can do wonders. Use a line of masking tape at the top of the lettering you are starting, and a line of tape at the bottom, to give you a clean letter height.

It takes a little time to set out faintly in pencil the spacing of the words and letters, but this preparation will greatly assist you in making a neat, professional-looking job.

Little signs made of wood are always popular, and supplies can be purchased at most hobby supply shops. A little assembling labor can transform them into saleable items.

If your yacht is large enough to install an engraving machine and a stock of sheet plastics of different colors, you are now open for business to make all kinds of nautical signs. Even complete new instrument panels can be manufactured professionally. With a real engraving machine there are many opportunities for making money, and you will be able to make your own sign, "Engravings Made To Order." Fortunately this is a skill that with the right equipment is more easily learned than engraving by hand.

If you are anchored or berthed near a local boatyard you can be of service to them when they have a call for a new instrument panel or other specialized signs. There are always trophies needing nameplates engraved; you can consult with the local schools or youth clubs, and maybe open the door for lots of money to be made.

Manufacturers of luxury yachts usually mark all kinds of things with plastic signs: 120-volt service, 12-volt service, fire extinguisher, fresh water, salt water, life preservers, flares inside locker, and many others. I once counted over thirty nameplates on a 55-foot Hatteras motor yacht, most of them weathered and cracked. These little nameplates deteriorate, especially in the sunshine, losing their color and cracking. Many owners will pay to have all the nameplates around their yacht replaced with new ones.

Boat Models For Sale

Enthusiastic boaters are often interested in purchasing a model or half model of their boat. The model has to resemble the customer's hull, and of course it has to be painted to match the hull's finish. Models and half models are always a saleable item, even to a local restaurant or business, to add a nautical touch or decoration hanging from the ceiling.

Hobby shops have materials that a person with woodworking skills can shape into a boat model. Hobby shops also have model kits that a person with time on his hands can assemble, and who can resist studying a model of Nelson's flagship or the *Cutty Sark* or another famous square-rigger with all her intricate rigging, masts, and sails. Though such models take many hours to complete and must be very well finished, they sell for very high prices.

FLAGS AND PENNANTS FOR SALE

If you acquire a sewing machine, especially a heavy-duty model capable of stitching sailcloth, you can make and sell all kinds of items.

You can make flags of different countries, researching the proper colors and styles from a book or from the Internet. You can make signal flags, often carried by sailors leaving to visit different foreign ports. (When you enter a foreign port, you must fly the yellow quarantine flag from the starboard spreader of the mainmast, and it is always expected that you will also fly the flag of the country you are visiting. The quarantine flag must be flown until the authorities have cleared you into their country. You must satisfy their immigration, customs and importing regulations. You may not go ashore or leave your boat for any reason until the authorities have said you are cleared to do so.) You may be commissioned to make a custom flag designed for a specific owner for his own boat.

With the sewing machine you can make sail covers, which are fairly simple, loose-fitting covers to keep the sun from damaging the sails when they are not in use.

You can make sun awnings, usually rectangles of material that lay over the boom and whose corners tie off to the standing rigging. Awnings, an absolute necessity for boats in the tropics, help keep the cabin cooler and provide shade for those in the cockpit when anchored.

Many boat owners have covers made for their dinghy, the stowed outboard motor, the deck hatches, the life raft, and the winches; even all the varnished wood is sometimes covered when the boat is not being used. Since varnish work needs to be refinished about every three months if under the tropic sun, it greatly cuts down on this maintenance if the varnished surfaces are covered.

As you get to be more experienced with the machine, you can

re-cover boat cushions and interior upholstery. Cockpit cushions are very popular, but they suffer most from the sun's damaging rays and thus need new covers more often.

You can even make sail repairs, though parts of the sails have so many layers of material that only the strongest commercial machines can sew these reinforced parts. Some hand stitching will also be needed for sail repairs.

You may also be able to splice rope, making loop ends and setting up boats properly in their berths. Skippers don't always take the time to fit their dock lines to their boat. If the lines are not set up right, it is necessary to retie the boat every time it returns to the berth. However, with loops spliced into the ends of the dock lines to loop over the boat's cleats, the other ends can be secured to the docks with the proper adjustment when the boat is exactly where you want it in the berth. Then when the boat comes back into the berth it is only a matter of looping the lines over the boat's cleats and the boat is now in the proper place in the berth and no adjusting of the lines is necessary.

Having the boat set up like this really simplifies its use.

If you have and can use a sewing machine, hang out your shingle, and you may find you are busier than you want to be. But you will still be operating away from the rat race, working at your own pace from your boat, with no commuting.

FISHING TACKLE

Maybe you are a skilled fisherman, able to make your own fishing tackle. There is a market for handmade tackle, especially if it is made with know-how after years of fishing experience. There are so many different types of fishing, and so many people want to fish who do not know exactly what tackle is best to use. If they are targeting a particular fish, they need to know the best approach or just the right way to rig their lines.

On my first trip to Tahiti, I had bought a large box of fishing tackle that we used every which way on the ocean, but to no avail. The tackle was obviously much too light for ocean fishing. We lost lure after lure, until most were gone.

After arriving in French Polynesia, we asked the storeowner what type of line and lure we needed. We were told to use 400-kilo line with large squid lures; then we would catch fish. That was 800-pound breaking strain line, the lures were almost a foot long, and the hooks were massive.

We did catch fish--mahi mahi, wahoo, yellow-fin tuna, even a great blue marlin--after we started using the correct tackle. If we had bought the right fishing gear from a knowledgeable fisherman in the first place, we almost certainly would have had many dinners of fresh fish. This also extends the cruising budget, and what a treat to have fish to eat the same day it is caught.

It has been my experience that fishermen will spend whatever it takes to buy tackle that catches fish regularly--and good lures are not cheap. If you know what equipment is necessary and can make good lures, there is a market for them.

DRIFTWOOD ART

Almost like treasure hunting, scouring the beaches for driftwood can be a lot of fun. Studying a piece to figure what it represents to you or what you can make out of it, is a challenge. The artist in you can make all sorts of driftwood art. With your boat you can reach beaches only accessible from the water, so it is an advantage being able to search for driftwood along a beach where very few people have a chance to walk.

The same applies to shell hunting, a most pleasant pastime whose finds are the material for making all kinds of ornaments. Driftwood can be adorned with shells to make interesting pieces, many of which could be sold to local shops, especially those frequented by tourists. With glue, shells can be put together in a myriad of ways to make little animals, brooches, necklaces, and adornments for dresses, hats, and so forth. Little night-lights can be made with a larger shell. Photograph holders are more interesting with a surrounding border of small shells, and colorful shells can brighten up ornaments in lots of ways.

When you live on your boat and have lots of time on your hands, the opportunity is there to find all kinds of seashore art. Spend a little time on it, and you have a saleable item. What an easy and fun way to make a little cash!

TREASURE HUNTING

Treasure hunting has a certain fascination for most of us. Even when you go exploring along a beach looking for shells or anything out of the ordinary, you are a mini treasure hunter. When you have a boat at your disposal, the possibilities are there to really go treasure hunting.

With a simple grapnel hook and a strong line, you can begin searching the bottom of bays where boats regularly anchor. You may be lucky and hook onto an anchor and chain that some sailor couldn't retrieve because it snagged on the bottom. Anchors and chains are very expensive and don't wear out, so are always worth money.

Of course we have all seen those folks with sounding devices scouring the beaches where people sunbathe. There is always the chance that a person has lost a ring or necklace in the sand or that cash has fallen out of someone's pockets. The possibilities are endless. Finders keep, losers weep.

There are many boats and ships lying on the bottom. These are documented with approximate positions listed, and those who search the records and enter upon an expedition to search for them may find treasure beyond belief. The treasure hunter Mel Fisher was extremely successful after many years of searching when he and his assistants found the Spanish Galleon *Atosca* lying on the bottom of the Caribbean Sea. Fisher and his crew took many, many millions of dollars worth of gold, diamonds, coin, jewelry, and artifacts from the wreck.

Of course, there are many treasure hunters who don't have the know-how or the luck of Mel Fisher, but everywhere there are sunken boats with marine equipment on the hulks, just waiting to be stripped. Anchors, winches, ropes, lines, chain, and most marine gear can withstand immersion in salt water for a long time without deteriorating.

A close friend of mine, sailing around the world a few years ago, sailed to Beveridge Reef in the South Pacific. He had read the account of an ill-fated yacht going aground on a reef to the north of Beveridge Reef, and felt the yacht may have gone aground on Beveridge Reef instead. The wreck had happened only the previous year. Sure enough, it was on the bottom of the lagoon of Beveridge; my friend and his wife found the wreck in only forty feet of water. After a few days of fun diving with scuba tanks, they had a host of valuable stuff to sell, all still in excellent condition.

Even if you don't find a fortune in gold treasure hunting, there is always the excitement of the hunt--and who knows, you might get lucky. However, you must be extremely cautious if wreck diving, for it can be very dangerous.

WRITING ARTICLES OF YOUR EXPERIENCES

Armchair travelers, even experienced and participating sailors, are always interested in reading about other people's travels. If the writer has researched the area and gives a lot of information regarding the geography, the culture, the history of the inhabitants, their language, temperament or style of the people visited, and other pertinent facts, it can be very enjoyable reading. It is especially interesting reading for a person contemplating a trip to the same place. It adds a lot of enjoyment to a vacation if you have been able to read something about the place before you go there.

If you have spent time in an unusual place, take the time to write about it. You don't have to be a literary genius, but just tell it like it is. Some of the most enjoyable reading is simply an account of another's experiences. My own travels to different parts of the world have certainly been spurred on by the accounts of others before me, describing their adventures.

You may find out that you have a talent for writing; you may even make a very successful livelihood traveling to different parts of the world, putting down on paper your experiences for others to enjoy also.

Though I have sailed almost thirty thousand miles across oceans, visiting many countries, I relish reading yachting magazines, each month devouring *Latitude 38* with its many articles about people cruising in different parts of the world. Even articles written about places where I have spent lots of time, interest me. Many publications are hungry for good travel articles. There is no end to the enjoyment one gets from reading of other people's adventures. There are articles written by travelers who have spent only a week or two in a place, yet the information makes for enjoyable reading.

Eric and Susan Hiscock spent their entire working lives living on boats, cruising around the world many times. All their expenses were paid for by the articles and books they wrote. Eric was an excellent photographer and processed his work in the forward cabin, which they had turned into a darkroom. His many books are most informative regarding cruising on small boats.

Photography at one time was very expensive; film had to be developed, and once the film was shot, that was it. Now, with video and digital cameras, the same tape can be reshot over and over again, 'till you get exactly the shot or movie you desire. It is more feasible now to make a video of any trip you take. You can come home with wonderful movies, even with perfect sound. Just don't move the camera all over the place like so many boring home movies that give a person a headache. You can even purchase a printer that can make a still photograph from any frame of your videotape to accompany the article you write.

You may find that you enjoy lecturing about your travels. Yacht clubs are good places to give a lecture or show sailing and boating videos.

PARTING THOUGHTS

Fishermen say that every day spent fishing prolongs your life by one day. I feel the same about boating.

In fact, a very good friend of mine, Bill, with his 36-foot steel yacht ready for the sail from California to Australia, had two stainless steel knees fitted to his legs, six months before departure. His recovery was so remarkable, the surgeon said, "I am going to recommend to all my patients that they go live on a boat."

Bill and his wife Gail left California in their mid-seventies, and though they had never crossed an ocean before, sailed by themselves all the way to Australia. I last heard from Bill when he phoned from Tasmania. He claimed that they were now in better shape physically than they had been in years.

I have never regretted the time I have spent in my life sailing, building boats, or cruising to faraway islands. Spending so much time boating, I may not have advanced my station in life financially, because I have never really been focused on just accumulating money, but I have enjoyed myself, and the healthy sea air may even have lengthened my days on this beautiful earth.

I know some who complain that our environment is completely destroyed. In fact a young man I had met who had started building a boat was so depressed about the things he was hearing about the state of the world, he committed suicide.

If he had finished his boat and gone out on the ocean, he would have found the waters offshore to be crystal clear, blue and full of wonderful things to see. The world is far from being finished, and there is health and beauty all around us.

I hope this book will inspire some would-be sailor to go do it. Even a small sailboat will open up the whole world to you.

Recommended Reading

Around The World in Wanderer 3, by Eric Hiscock.
Cruising Under Sail, by Eric Hiscock.
Gipsy Moth Circles the World, by Sir Francis Chichester.
Great Voyages in Small Boats, by John De Graff. This includes
"The voyages of John Guzzwell" and "Trekka Round the World,"
by Vito Dumas, as well as "Alone through the Roaring Forties" and
"Sailing Alone Around the World," by Joshua Slocum
Oceanography and Seamanship. By William G. Van Dorn.
The Living Sea, by Captain J. Y. Cousteau.
The Macmillan Book of Boating, by William N. Wallace.
The Ocean Sailing Yacht, by Donald M Street, Jr.
The Proper Yacht, by Arthur Beiser.
The Proper Yacht, second edition, by Arthur Beiser.
Tahiti, Romance and Reality, by James Siers
Voyaging Under Sail, by Eric Hiscock.

There are, of course, countless other books on this subject, many of
them excellent manuscripts full of information and with enough lure
to excite many a heart already longing for far horizons.